The Future of
National Intelligence

SECURITY AND PROFESSIONAL INTELLIGENCE EDUCATION SERIES (SPIES)

Series Editor: Jan Goldman

In this post–September 11, 2001, era there has been rapid growth in the number of professional intelligence training and educational programs across the United States and abroad. Colleges and universities, as well as high schools, are developing programs and courses in homeland security, intelligence analysis, and law enforcement, in support of national security.

The Security and Professional Intelligence Education Series (SPIES) was first designed for individuals studying for careers in intelligence and to help improve the skills of those already in the profession; however, it was also developed to educate the public on how intelligence work is conducted and should be conducted in this important and vital profession.

Books in this series:

Communicating with Intelligence: Writing and Briefing in the Intelligence and National Security Communities, by James S. Major. 2008.

A Spy's Résumé: Confessions of a Maverick Intelligence Professional and Misadventure Capitalist, by Marc Anthony Viola. 2008.

An Introduction to Intelligence Research and Analysis, by Jerome Clauser, revised and edited by Jan Goldman. 2008.

Writing Classified and Unclassified Papers for National Security, by James S. Major. 2009.

Strategic Intelligence: A Handbook for Practitioners, Managers, and Users, revised edition by Don McDowell. 2009.

Partly Cloudy: Ethics in War, Espionage, Covert Action, and Interrogation, by David L. Perry. 2009.

Tokyo Rose/An American Patriot: A Dual Biography, by Frederick P. Close. 2010.

Ethics of Spying: A Reader for the Intelligence Professional, edited by Jan Goldman. 2006.

Ethics of Spying: A Reader for the Intelligence Professional, Volume 2, edited by Jan Goldman. 2010.

A Woman's War: The Professional and Personal Journey of the Navy's First African American Female Intelligence Officer, by Gail Harris. 2010.

Handbook of Scientific Methods of Inquiry for Intelligence Analysis, by Hank Prunckun. 2010.

Handbook of Warning Intelligence: Assessing the Threat to National Security, by Cynthia Grabo. 2010.

Keeping U.S. Intelligence Effective: The Need for a Revolution in Intelligence Affairs, by William J. Lahneman. 2011.

Words of Intelligence: An Intelligence Professional's Lexicon for Domestic and Foreign Threats, Second Edition, by Jan Goldman. 2011.

Counterintelligence Theory and Practice, by Hank Prunckun. 2012.

Balancing Liberty and Security: An Ethical Study of U.S. Foreign Intelligence Surveillance, 2001–2009, by Michelle Louise Atkin. 2013.

The Art of Intelligence: Simulations, Exercises, and Games, edited by William J. Lahneman and Rubén Arcos. 2014.

Communicating with Intelligence: Writing and Briefing in National Security, by James S. Major. 2014.

Scientific Methods of Inquiry for Intelligence Analysis, Second Edition, by Hank Prunckun. 2014.

Quantitative Intelligence Analysis: Applied Analytic Models, Simulations, and Games, by Edward Waltz. 2014.

The Handbook of Warning Intelligence: Assessing the Threat to National Security—The Complete Declassified Edition, by Cynthia Grabo. 2015.

Intelligence and Information Policy for National Security: Key Terms and Concepts, by Jan Goldman and Susan Maret. 2016.

Handbook of European Intelligence Cultures, edited by Bob de Graaff and James M. Nyce, with Chelsea Locke. 2016.

Partly Cloudy: Ethics in War, Espionage, Covert Action, and Interrogation, Second Edition, by David L. Perry. 2016.

Humanitarian Intelligence: A Practitioner's Guide to Crisis Analysis and Project Design, by Andrej Zwitter. 2016.

Shattered Illusions: KGB Cold War Espionage in Canada, by Donald G. Mahar. 2016.

Intelligence Engineering: Operating Beyond the Conventional, by Adam D. M. Svendsen. 2017.

Reasoning for Intelligence Analysts: A Multidimensional Approach of Traits, Techniques, and Targets, by Noel Hendrickson. 2018.

Counterintelligence Theory and Practice, Second Edition, by Hank Prunckun. 2019.

Methods of Inquiry for Intelligence Analysis, Third Edition, by Hank Prunckun. 2019.

Weaponized Marketing: Defeating Radical Islam with Marketing That Built the World's Top Brands, by Lisa Merriam and Milton Kotler. 2020.

Shadow Warfare: Cyberwar Policy in the United States, Russia and China, by Elizabeth Van Wie Davis. 2021.

The Future of National Intelligence

How Emerging Technologies Reshape Intelligence Communities

Shay Hershkovitz

ROWMAN & LITTLEFIELD
Lanham • Boulder • New York • London

Published by Rowman & Littlefield
An imprint of The Rowman & Littlefield Publishing Group, Inc.
4501 Forbes Boulevard, Suite 200, Lanham, Maryland 20706
www.rowman.com

86-90 Paul Street, London EC2A 4NE, United Kingdom

British Library Cataloguing in Publication Information Available

Library of Congress Cataloging-in-Publication Data

Names: Hershkovitz, Shay, 1976– author.
Title: The future of national intelligence: how emerging technologies reshape
    intelligence communities / Shay Hershkovitz.
Description: Lanham, Maryland: Rowman & Littlefield, 2022. | Series: Security and
    professional intelligence education series; 37 | Includes bibliographical references
    and index. | Summary: "The Future of National Intelligence: How Emerging
    Technologies Reshape Intelligence Communities provides a blueprint for the future of
    national intelligence agencies by exploring emerging technologies and collaborative
    strategies for intelligence gathering and managing data"—Provided by publisher.
Identifiers: LCCN 2022008551 (print) | LCCN 2022008552 (ebook)
    | ISBN 9781538160695 (cloth) | ISBN 9781538160701 (paperback)
    | ISBN 9781538160718 (epub)
Subjects: LCSH: Intelligence service—Technological innovations. | Intelligence
    service—Western countries. | Intelligence Service—International cooperation.
Classification: LCC JF1525.I6 H479 2022 (print) | LCC JF1525.I6
    (ebook) | DDC 327.120285/4678—dc23/eng/20220701
LC record available at https://lccn.loc.gov/2022008551
LC ebook record available at https://lccn.loc.gov/2022008552

Contents

Foreword

The environment in which intelligence communities (ICs) in the West operate has been experiencing continuous multifaceted dramatic change that requires a revolution in the way intelligence organizations perform. Some of the change has to do with the nature of adversaries. Even as ICs must keep a watchful eye on rival states and contend with strategic weapons proliferation, new challenges have been added. Hybrid terror organizations and other nonstate actors pose a major challenge with low visibility and different hurdles to overcome in understanding their ideology and modus operandi and gaining access to their secrets. Cyber activity is used for distortion, denying vital access to information and services, espionage, and influencing the democratic political process. At the same time, ICs have to deal with such unfamiliar threats to national security as climate change and pandemics.

On top of the change in the nature of the subjects that ICs have to deal with has been a rapid change in the technologies relevant to intelligence and a revolution in the characteristics of the data it deals with, as well as associated technologies (e.g., big data, artificial intelligence, the growing importance of open sources, social media, and more). Unlike in the past, most of the technological breakthroughs are carried out in the private sector by giant corporations, as well as small start-ups. Moreover, the new generation of experts has a different approach to mobility in their career development. The challenge of ICs becomes even greater as they lose the monopoly on providing information and analysis to decision makers and the "fake news" phenomenon makes it more difficult to determine what is reality. The characteristics of the recipients of the intelligence have changed, too, and beyond the well-known policy and military decision makers are new nonmilitary consumers and the general public. Further, the IC itself has become a major consumer as more campaigns and operations are executed, and sometimes led, by intelligence organizations.

These developments require significant changes in the IC itself, including adapting the process of intelligence production to the technological changes, building agile interfaces with the business sector, integrating the community into a joint ecosystem with it, developing new approaches to employing adequate people, and relying more on open sources in the broad meaning of this term. The IC should also broaden its capability to perform its operational functions, including in the cyber domain. It should develop proper tools to perform its duties in the context of protecting the democratic process against fake news and foreign intervention. It should make the adjustments needed to enable it to deal with new topics and new consumers from outside the national security community. Most of all, it must improve its learning process and keep incentivizing and promoting innovations to make it able to cope with the growing pace of change and increase jointness among its various components within each agency, between them, and beyond, so that all its capabilities are fully used to produce the best intelligence.

A major topic that is a common denominator of these changes is how they affect the people involved in the process of producing intelligence on all agencies and all professions. A crucial question is how the role of the "man in the loop" will be affected by the growing capabilities of technology that may replace intelligence manpower and even considerably improve their efficacy. In *The Future of National Intelligence*, Dr. Shay Hershkovitz looks deep into this issue, analyzes the impact of the technological and data revolutions on the profession of intelligence and the people who work in the IC, and foresees what the new and important role of IC experts will look like. This is a must-read book for anyone interested in the future of intelligence and the relations between technology and human beings in general.

Brig. General (Ret.) Yossi Kuperwasser
Director
Intelligence Methodology Research Institute,
Israeli Intelligence Community Commemoration Center

Introduction

Technology and Systemic Change

It was a cold November morning in 1994. I was sitting on a military bus with a bunch of other eighteen-year-olds waiting to be sent to basic training camp. I looked outside the window. My mother waved at me with tears in her eyes. I had very little idea of what the future held for me.

Like most Israelis, after finishing high school, I was drafted into the Israel Defense Forces (IDF). As I had learned Arabic in school and had a strong affinity to geopolitics, especially Middle Eastern geopolitics, I was assigned to the military intelligence corps.

I still remember the day I was given access to one of the terminals my unit used to consume sensitive information. It was a Vax workstation with a monochromatic green screen. Nothing fancy. No multimedia. Just endless lines of text. But I was fascinated. Here I was, an eighteen-year-old who had just finished high school, and I was about to enter the world of shadows—the world of John le Carré, James Bond, and the famous Israeli spy Eli Cohen. I felt ready. I was about to become a spy.

It was then that my long journey with intelligence began, although at the time I thought it was just my military assignment. I left the Israeli intelligence community (IC) after almost fifteen years and pursued a career in management consulting and market research while keeping a foot in academia as an adjunct professor at various universities. But you know what they say: you can leave the world of intelligence, but intelligence never leaves you. Throughout the years I have followed the field of intelligence studies and worked with national security organizations worldwide, this time as an outsider.

I have worked on dozens of what I call "future of" studies. Some of these studies were related to national security, but most of them dealt with less-exciting aspects of human life, including the future of money, health care, and insurance. At about the same time I started working as the head of research at the XPRIZE Foundation, I became more and more intrigued by cutting-edge emerging technologies, especially artificial intelligence (AI). It wasn't just an intellectual curiosity: given that I managed a large team of analysts, and as my team was required to address multiple topics simultaneously and produce comprehensive reports, I realized that maybe I should find better, more efficient ways to conduct these studies. Don't get me wrong: my team was composed of many highly talented individuals, but I kept wondering how I could best use this valuable resource. How could I allow them to focus on what they did best, all while delivering projects on time, on budget, and without compromising on scientific rigor?

At XPRIZE we didn't use Vax or similar platforms. We used laptops. We used Google. The entire world was at our fingertips. But how could we perform better and more efficiently? I figured that AI was the answer. Why not let people do what they do best—hypothesizing and reasoning—and let computers do what they do best—mainly, quickly collecting and analyzing large databases? This, I reasoned, would allow my team to focus on analysis rather than sifting through endless amounts of data. It was then that my new romance began—I simply fell in love with the potential of AI and started exploring its potential for research and analysis purposes.

At some point I started pondering, what if intelligence analysts could also use such platforms? Being the geek that I am, I started researching the topic. AI led me to explore big data, then quantum computing, then blockchain. I felt like I had discovered a new world after spending so many years in confined environments (intelligence and academia are more similar than people realize). I was completely blind to the exciting technological developments of recent years. "I am going to write a book on the future of intelligence," I told myself. "I wonder how intelligence professionals see the future of their profession. Maybe I should start asking them."

That's how my journey began, and here we are.

Like some of the "future of intelligence" studies, I am interested in learning how emerging technology will change intelligence. But unlike these studies, I am more focused on long-term broader and deeper changes. I believe that if we really want to learn what intelligence and especially national intelligence will look like, we must look outside the national security establishment—that is, we should explore not only what governments are doing, but also, more important, what is happening in the private sector and academia. And great things are happening there.

We live in an age of exponential technologies—technologies that, until recently, were science fiction. And they are already changing how we carry out national intelligence. Take, for example, AI, which is already transforming the way we collect and analyze information. Or robots, which we're using to create new types of intelligence products. Or virtual reality, which can simulate the most challenging environments in which intelligence agents operate. Or synthetic biology and 3-D printing, which have already created new types of threats.

This book, however, doesn't focus on these and other new threats but, rather, on the technologies that are shaping how intelligence is done. In that respect, I see eight key technologies already transforming national intelligence. The first two, the Internet of Things (IoT) and 5G technology, will elevate the mobile network to not only interconnect people, but also interconnect and control machines, objects, and devices. That, in turn, will create even more data, taking big data, the third, to the next level. Fourth, cloud computing and storage will not only allow for a much greater computing power, but also, not least important, force intelligence organizations to divorce their highly protective, siloed approach when it comes to storing data. Fifth, of course, is the queen of technologies—AI—which is already applied in most facets of intelligence work. Sixth, blockchain is another key technology, essentially alien to how intelligence organizations should be structured and operated, because this technology cherishes the concept of decentralized control of data. Seventh, and farther into the future, quantum computing will take computing power to an entirely new level. And finally, albeit not really a technology, crowdsourcing represents another aspect of decentralization—this time decentralization of knowledge.

But do intelligence professionals realize the magnitude of the change?

At a conference on the future challenges of intelligence organizations held in 2018, the former U.S. director of national intelligence, Dan Coats, argued that the transformation of the American IC must be a *revolution* rather than an *evolution*. The community must be innovative and flexible, capable of rapidly adopting innovative technologies wherever they may arise. As we shall see, although many past and present intelligence professionals do acknowledge the need for their organizations to change, Coats represents a somewhat unique voice, as too often people talk about the need to change, but what they really mean is that ICs need to adjust, not necessarily transform.

I argue that ICs in the Western world are now at a crossroads; the growing proliferation of the aforementioned technologies changes the rules of the game. Thus, it isn't surprising that intelligence organizations are now struggling with truths that have historically shaped their endeavors. The hierarchical, compartmentalized, industrial structure of these organizations is now changing, revolving primarily around the integration of new technologies with traditional intelligence work and the redefinition of the role of the humans in the intelligence process.

One might argue that technology and intelligence have always gone hand in hand, and this age is no different than previous technological revolutions that affected ICs. Take, for example, World War I, when cameras were put on the newly developed aerial platforms, creating a new intelligence discipline, VISINT—visual intelligence. The early version of Go-Pro, if you will. Or, in World War II, the early versions of computers, and especially computer-based encryption, leapfrogged when British intelligence deciphered the sophisticated German encryption machine, Enigma. They were the first hackers. And later, in the early days of the Cold War, the Central Intelligence Agency and U.S. Air Force developed satellites and high-altitude jets, paving the way for a massive civil use of satellites—such as Waze or Google Maps.

So, yes, technology and intelligence have always gone hand in hand; technology changed intelligence, and intelligence organizations developed new technologies that later became widespread. But despite these fascinating technological developments, intelligence organizations kept following one *basic* idea: the intelligence cycle.

Professor Sherman Kent created the concept of the intelligence cycle in the early 1950s, and it reflected an assembly-line kind of logic: intelligence work starts with the needs of the consumers of intelligence, the policy makers. The IC then collects information according to those needs, analyzes the information gathered, produces deliverables based on that analysis, disseminates those deliverables to the consumers, and receives their feedback, and the cycle starts all over again.

That's how most agencies have worked; and despite many technological breakthroughs since the 1950s, that's how they still work (at least notionally). Several people I interviewed for this book argued that the intelligence cycle is more of a concept rather than a real practice. That might be the case, but the fact that the intelligence cycle is still being used as the organizing principle of intelligence work, for example, differentiating collection and analysis or creating a metaphoric wall separating decision makers (too often called consumers of intelligence) from intelligence professionals, represents a philosophy and practice that no longer adhere to our changing world and need to be replaced with new concepts. Such concepts will diverge from seeing each part or function in the cycle as isolated and compartmentalized from one another.

Luckily, we see how this is slowly changing.

In recent years, the discourse on the future of intelligence has been growing and developing in different directions. Discussions have ranged from how certain technologies will be affected by specific fields—for example, how AI and image processing will affect the war on terror—to more abstract issues. The latter include, for instance, the analyst's place in the future research process or the development of various approaches and methodologies relevant to the information age—the creation of new intelligence disciplines or concepts that will replace the idea of the intelligence cycle, for instance.

THE NEED FOR A SYSTEMIC FRAMEWORK

Various theories have been proposed to explain how technology prompts organizational change, but in general they have either focused on the technology and ignored the influence of human agency or on social interaction and structure and ignored the technology.

This book focuses on technology as the driving force that requires intelligence organizations (as part of the national security establishment) to radically transform themselves. It does not, however, see technology as the only driving force; and it does not see technology only as the driver of such transformation, but also as its enabler. By differentiating "driver" and "enabler," I refer to a distinction, crucial for this book, between an organization and its environment.

The purpose of this book is not to add theoretical layers to any organizational theories, regardless of their school of thought; however, that does not mean that this book lacks theoretical foundation. In fact, the theoretical foundations are what determined anything related to the research: the research question, the entities I decided to focus on, the types of sources I use, the interpretation of the finding, and the most fundamental principles of intelligence transformation that are presented in the final chapter.

For now, I will suffice by saying that I see the intelligence establishment as a social system. A "system" is a combination of different components operating within a certain environment. Each component has its own traits and functions. Yet, their interaction has an effect on the entire complex, and they work together under a common goal. This goal predefines the total achievement to which the actions of the system aspire; it also regulates and organizes the relations between the various components, as well as the sum of the system's relation with its surroundings. Between the components of the system—themselves composed of sub-elements—exists an inherent tension linking the system's action toward that at which they are aimed and their independent goals. This tension, when reflecting a similarity between the system goal and the aims of the components actions, allows operationalization of the system's goal with the practical actions leading to its achievement.[1]

Now let's return to technology. The literature is chock-full of different perspectives of the effect technology has on organizations. Brevity prevents me from discussing the differences and similarities between these theories. I will suffice by arguing that some theories—for example, structuration theory or actor network theory—tend to focus on the actions of agents but ignore technology, whereas institutional theories tend to ignore agency and focus on technology or other external stimuli. Further, technology itself is often treated as a unitary object, ignoring each technology's distinctive characteristics.

This book tries to avoid that theoretical pitfall: first, it focuses on the resonance technology causes while being aware that other types of stimuli are in the environment in which the IC system exists. Second, it addresses specific technologies separately—for instance, AI or big data—and discusses their effect on the various facets of intelligence work. Third, and probably most important, this book argues that to fully understand the magnitude of the change, one cannot discuss these technologies as singletons: they are codependent and affect one another. Fourth, it does not focus only on technology but, rather, explores how technology affects a multitude of intelligence components, from structures to the individuals performing intelligence work. It also avoids discussion of how specific disciplines and their organizational manifestations (e.g., collection disciplines and units) are affected by the technological changes, because it tries to present a comprehensive look at how a subset of the national security establishment—that is, the IC—is changing.

METHODOLOGICAL FRAMEWORK

The current work brings together three content worlds, two of which are generally covered in the literature on the future of intelligence—technological advances and the intelligence profession. The third involves the ways in which technological innovations are driven by the private sector. As such, the research extends beyond the techno-intelligence world to examine products that are already available or in development, and that are used in other fields—for example, market research, marketing and sales, and supply chain management. The starting point for the analysis is the leading technological trends in the private market and their implications for intelligence services.

The purpose of this study is to examine the manner in which technologies will affect national intelligence. The underlying research question is as follows: In what ways will emerging technologies change the intelligence profession? Almost every word in this research question needs clarification: What technologies can be defined as emerging? What does the term "intelligence profession" mean, and how do we define change? What aspects of the profession change as a result of technological developments? Further, how can emerging technologies be isolated as an (independent) variable that affects the intelligence (dependent) variable? In general, is it possible to consider the relationship as one-directional (technology affects intelligence) in an era in which the relationships between intelligence activity and the public and private sectors are indistinct, and is it difficult to define what came first?

However, the discussion here has been limited to a well-defined sphere: how specific technologies have made a quantum leap in recent years, affecting the core issues of the intelligence profession—research, data collection, the range of intelligence disciplines, organizational structures, and the place of the individual (the intelligence professional) in this complex structure.

The main argument at the heart of this book is that in the post-industrial age, thanks to easier and affordable data capture, storage, and computing power, agencies now have competition in collecting information. Policy makers now need the agencies to focus on making sense of the huge quantities of data available. But to get there, agencies must free themselves of their industrial-era assumptions. They need new definitions of secrets, and they must open themselves up to collaboration with outsiders. Beyond these immediate concerns, they must adjust to broader notions of national security, no longer limited to the conventional and nonconventional powers of states and nonstate actors. Agencies must address technological supremacy, climate change, and the global flow of people, goods, and information. We are now living in a broad-based technological arms race, with implications far beyond the military domain. These technologies are already transforming society, and agencies must, in turn, transform their operations to keep up, not only the process of data collection and analysis, but also their internal structure, recruitment, relations with policy makers, and ties to outside resources.

I am aware of the variety of possibilities for describing change to intelligence institutions. This study is specifically limited to an examination of the interaction between technology and intelligence, and mainly looks at the intelligence system inward—how the system perceives the environment in which it operates; the way it is structured and organized; and the ways in which it produces outputs. I also refer, albeit in somewhat limited capacity, to how technology changes the interaction of the intelligence system with the environment, given the assumption that to describe this stage, the study should examine how technological developments affect aspects far beyond those that have immediate implications for intelligence, or at least changes in perceptions and systems of national security.

We have two additional and similar methodological challenges: First is the difficulty of discussing one technology without referring to the other—a reflection of the trend of convergence (the integration of technologies, products, and services). Second is the difficulty of deconstructing the intelligence profession into distinct components—including distinguishing between collecting, researching, producing, and disseminating intelligence products—especially when one of the central arguments in this work is that the relevance of the traditional divisions between these intelligence fields has been eroded. The combination of technological convergence and intelligence convergence leaves us, therefore, not only with a methodological problem, but even worse, with a conceptual problem that presents as a terminological problem. How can we take apart and reassemble the intelligence profession in a coherent way? What terms will we use? Will we invent a new language?

To overcome these obstacles, I have used several artificial divisions: First, I present a number of technologies in an integrated manner (big data, AI, data storage, computing power, and robotics) because I believe that fully understanding these technologies and their future effect requires that they are considered holistically. In other cases, I present specific emerging technologies in isolated form, although it is clear that these technologies rely on others. Second, I consider how each such technological combination, as well as isolated technologies, affects national intelligence; and I deal mainly with the collection, research, and development of the intelligence product, in an attempt to describe these three components as a whole. Third, I present several broad intelligence issues, such as the intelligence–decision-maker nexus or the privatization of intelligence; and discuss the changes they will experience without referring to one specific technology. Finally, I generally use familiar concepts, critique them, and imbue them with new meanings, rather than inventing new concepts.

This study uses several types of information sources, a combination that allows, I hope, the representation of the future of intelligence from a rich and diverse perspective. First, I use two types of secondary sources: those that deal with technology and those that discuss the effect of technology on intelligence. I have not limited myself to academic literature but, rather, have expanded the sources to publications by government agencies, research institutes, corporations, and other institutions, as well as market research from markets in which the relevant technologies are dominant. Second, I use five types of primary sources: (1) sites and publications by research and development bodies (security and intelligence) to identify the areas where resources are invested to generate breakthroughs; (2) sites, publications, and exhibitions showing relevant technological developments, including but not limited to companies offering services that can be termed "intelligence"—here I focus on the development centers of the giant corporations, start-ups, and venture capital funds that support them to identify future development directions; (3) interviews with entrepreneurs engaged in these technologies; (4) interviews with past intelligence professionals; and (5) interviews with companies that provide techno-intelligence services.

STRUCTURE OF THIS BOOK

Intelligence and Technology in Historical Context. Chapter 1 describes the evolution of national intelligence organizations with attention to technological developments. Rather than a comprehensive historic review, I chose to tell the story of the national intelligence establishment through the lens of technological development and to show how until the past few decades, intelligence organizations drove innovation.

New and Emerging Threats. Chapter 2 describes three new threats ICs increasingly face—threats that are closely associated with the technologies described in this book: first, the struggle over the hearts and minds of citizens in Western democracies mainly through manipulation of information and dissemination of disinformation: second, the technological arms race, aimed at gaining supremacy, or at least dominance, as a fundamental component of national security policy; and third, the growing threats to human security, mainly due to climate change and epidemics—two types of global crises with long-term implications that pose a significant threat to national security.

The Challenge to Intelligence Organizations. Chapter 3 discusses the challenges the new technologies pose for intelligence organizations and the discourse around the need for intelligence organizations to change. It explores why, unlike previous eras, the current one is unique and requires a fundamental transformation; analyzes the key challenges ICs now face (e.g., data flood, loss of supremacy over knowledge); explains why the traditional concept of the intelligence cycle is obsolete; and calls for the adoption of new, more relevant, concepts for intelligence agencies.

Emerging Technologies and the National Intelligence Enterprise. Chapter 4 delves into the issues detailed in chapter 3 with details on specific technologies: the Internet of Things, cloud computing and cloud storage, big data and AI, and crowdsourcing. It also explores the trajectories of technologies such as blockchain and quantum computing and their effect on intelligence work and structures.

Intelligence Professionals and Decision Makers: A Collaborative Approach. Chapter 5 examines the main approaches to interrelations between leadership and intelligence—the traditional approaches and the approach I have termed the "collaborative approach." I argue that in light of challenges ICs now face, the most effective way to cultivate knowledge required for policy is through a collaborative approach that brings together intelligence personnel and policy makers.

Opening the Closed Intelligence System. Chapter 6 addresses several aspects of the need to blur the boundaries between intelligence communities and other actors in their environment, primarily the private sector and academia. It also describes the privatization of some intelligence operations, including sensitive ones, the "intelligence" role that the media, groups, and individuals have taken on, and the efforts of intelligence agencies to open direct channels of communication with the public.

Intelligence and Civic Engagement: Emphasizing Collaboration. In chapter 7, I present two new approaches to enhance intelligence work in light of the technological (and other) trends presented in this book. I argue that intelligence efforts can enlist outsiders to help collect and process data, thus turning ordinary citizens into "prosumers" who blur the divide between the producers (intelligence professionals) and the consumers (the general public). Crowdsourced intelligence, or CROSINT, takes this work on a much larger scale by allowing groups of people to collaborate with agencies.

TEMPINT: A New Intelligence Paradigm. Chapter 8 tackles the outdated intelligence cycle by discussing two relatively new alternative concepts to the intelligence cycle: activity-based intelligence (ABI) and object-based production. It then presents a new concept that ICs should adopt, even if just as a tool for better conceptualization of intelligence work. TEMPINT, or temporal intelligence, is a new holistic approach to data collection, processing, and analysis.

Intelligence in the Time of COVID-19. Chapter 9 analyzes the role intelligence communities have undertaken in the fight against the virus amid a global pandemic. It explores most of the topics previously discussed in the context of COVID-19. It then presents the main lessons learned from the Israeli intelligence community's involvement in fighting the virus on a national scale.

The Five Cs of Intelligence Transformation. Finallly, chapter 10 distills the key principles for digitally transforming intelligence agencies. It presents the concept of the five Cs of intelligence transformation—principles that stand at the core of the much-needed revolution in intelligence affairs: connection, collaboration, critique, creativity, and content expertise.

Chapter 1

Intelligence and Technology in Historical Context

This book argues that current and emerging digital technologies are so pervasive and so comprehensive that intelligence organizations must transform themselves to stay relevant to policy makers. They must alter their fundamental structures and policies in a radical, not evolutionary, way.

The evolution of intelligence organizations can be described in many ways. One such story is of a reaction to the changes in the institutions of war, including the development and transformation of armies or military doctrines. Another is describing the change as a result of the expansion of national security establishments or changes in the decision-making structures and processes at the national level. But we can also describe the history of intelligence as a reaction of the intelligence system to technological changes—so long as we remember that the relationship between intelligence and technology goes both ways: intelligence is influenced by technological changes, but it also affects such changes. Clearly, the analysis of developments in intelligence from the limited perspective of technological change is lacking, because neither intelligence nor technology operates in a vacuum; each always reflects what happens in the political, economic, social, and other systems that shape modern society.

To advance this argument, it's helpful to start with how intelligence organizations have responded to technological change in the past. This is by no means a comprehensive review of the history of intelligence in modern times but, rather, an attempt to put the current—and much needed—transformation in a historic context. This chapter, therefore, will briefly touch on the most critical technology-driven changes agencies have faced and review how they have reacted amid those changes.

It is important to keep in mind the theoretical foundations—that is, describing intelligence communities or organizations as social systems.[1] Technological changes, therefore, are presented here as a resonance or

1

stimulation created in the intelligence system's environment, bringing about
the need of the systems to reevaluate (i.e., reinterpret) the context in which
the system operates. That, in turn, has led to certain changes in the system
and its components—most notably, by increasing their internal complexity to adhere to the increasing external complexity (driven and manifested
by technology).

The system and subsystems' reactions should be perceived as changes in
their institutional infrastructure that, in turn, constitute how the system perceived itself and interpreted internal and external co-occurrences. I will also
focus on the super-system itself, rather than its components, though I will
present examples that pertain to components and individuals.

As we shall also see, the IC has been characterized by both its reactive and
proactive nature to tackling technological changes: reactive, because—as
often happens with large government organizations—understanding, interpreting, and acting upon a change is always a slow, cumbersome process.
But they were also proactive, because for the better part of the twentieth
century, the agencies themselves introduced new technologies. Therefore,
it was easier for them to transform once they introduced a new technology.
Finally—and probably the most important argument of this chapter—one
basic logic remained almost untouched from the late 1940s to our time: that
of the intelligence cycle.

I focus on British developments up to World War II and American developments thereafter. These were the leading intelligence bodies in their respec-
tive time periods, and they paved the way for other Western countries, if not
the rest of the intelligence world.

PRE-MODERN INTELLIGENCE

If we define intelligence loosely as collecting and analyzing data and creating knowledge required for decisions related to national security, then intelligence has been around since ancient times. The biblical book of Joshua
describes spies sent to gather information about the land of Canaan[2]; then
Joshua son of Nun secretly sent two spies from Shittim. "Go, look over the
land," he said, "especially Jericho."

Ample evidence shows that the armies of the Greek and Roman empires
used (combat) intelligence functions[3]—as did armies around the world
in later times. More modern intelligence functions, though still far from
today's practices, developed coincident with the industrial revolution,
Western imperialism, and the rise of the nation-state. The innovations of the
industrial revolution drove the development of these functions: high-flying
hot-air balloons, binoculars, and telegraphs all provided new channels for

data collection beyond the reliance on spies or scouts. The refinement of typewriters and developments in the field of invisible ink facilitated the rapid and discreet transmission of information; and the increased newspaper circulation increased the potential inherent in open information. The expanding array of foreign attachés prompted cooperation on intelligence matters across countries.

The massive increase in the size of armies, mainly due to the dramatic changes in Napoleon's military organization, also contributed to the development of the intelligence profession. Moreover, Napoleon redefined the principles by which armies were organized; his approaches marked the entry of military thought and practice into the modern era. The talented French general used conscription to turn his forces into a people's army, alongside a massive, usually forced, mobilization of soldiers from captured nations or allies. He led an exponential expansion of armies as well as extending their campaign over time and space. By better mobilizing the nation's resources for war, he could fight more battles, longer, and over a broader area.[4]

Because war became more complex, systematic war planning, with strategic and operational plans, became critical in coordinating the various elements of military power. This, in turn, has led to the desire of enemies to obtain those plans by means of intelligence, such as espionage. Nevertheless, intelligence until the nineteenth century remained largely limited to the collection and processing of data for internal security purposes, such as protection of the leader and his family; as well as for collecting combat-related information, usually tactical, over the course of conflicts. Data collection methods primarily relied on spies, scouts, diplomats, the military attaché, and on open, journalistic sources.

Awareness of what is now known as "information security" was negligible. Take, for example, *The Times* of London, which provided valuable information to the Russian intelligence services during the Crimean War (1853–1856), including the scope and deployment of the British forces participating in the war, and even their operational plans.[5] Only in 1889 did the British enact the Official Secret Act, which defined penalties for those who leaked military information.

A milestone in the development of intelligence services was the Second Boer War (1899–1902), a series of military confrontations between the British Empire and the independent republics established by the Boers—Dutch, French, and German Protestant peasants who colonized South Africa from the seventeenth century. Prior to the Boer War, the British army tended to organize intelligence activities ad hoc, with the goal of providing commanders in the field with the information they required in battle. These activities were managed not by a designated intelligence function, but within other military functions.

For example, the Department of Topography & Statistics was a function established in the British Army in India in 1854 by engineering officials. It was responsible, among other things, for collecting and disseminating tactical information, such as field and population data.[6] And these intelligence activities were not constant but, rather, were implemented only during conflicts.

That changed during the Boer War, when several functions were created to collect data: primarily, combat intelligence officers assigned to combat units and intelligence officers assigned to headquarters and staff. It was then that electric interception (later called signal intelligence, or SIGINT) made its debut. The British Navy and Army had installed means of wireless communication on their ships and field units. The Boers were able to intercept some of that communication, making them the pioneers in signal intelligence.[7]

The multitude of information raised a new need: establishment of a central function to manage the analysis and dissemination of the great quantities of data that began to accumulate. Indeed, this change was not motivated by dramatic new technologies, but after the war, the British retained some of these new intelligence structures. The field intelligence units were dismantled as always, but the Ministry of Defence kept a small intelligence department. This office focused on collecting data about Germany, to the dismay of many British government officials reluctant to take this "ungentlemanly" step. The Office of the Admiralty also retained a small intelligence function, and the two departments dealt mainly with collecting open data, as well as information from British military attachés in Europe. Slowly, an intelligence system was starting to morph.

With growing fear over the German military buildup and German espionage on British soil, the United Kingdom took a fundamental step further. The government established a Secret Service Bureau to fight against foreign intelligence and collect information about the kingdom's potential enemies from secret sources. The bureau had an army section for preventing internal espionage and a naval section for collecting foreign intelligence. In 1916, the sections were expanded into two departments: Directorate of Military Intelligence Section 5 and Directorate of Military Intelligence Section 6. Over the years, these became the United Kingdom's two central intelligence agencies: MI-5 and MI-6. To complement those agencies with more tactical information, an intelligence force was set up within the British Army prior to the outbreak of World War I. Thus, the arms race (mainly technological) in Europe served as a catalyst for the improvement of the British and German intelligence institutions, bringing about an intelligence system with coherent goals and supporting subsystems.

Several approaches identify milestones in the development of intelligence organizations prior to World War II. One is that of Gregory F. Treverton, former chair of the U.S. National Intelligence Council, which holds that the first great revolution of intelligence took place in the transition of military thought from the conception of the French general Henri de Jomini (1779–1869) to the Prussian general Carl von Clausewitz (1780–1831).[8] Others believe that World War I, including the lead-up to that war, was when the first dramatic intelligence revolution took place: This was the first "total war," which required complete mobilization of the nation's resources; and it involved significant technological innovations on the battlefield, including battle aircraft and improved communication and encryption tools, which led to interception of communications and code breaking.

For example, during the war, the British security forces had two separate offices dealing with the production of intelligence through interception of calls and transmissions: the War Office operated the British Military Intelligence Section 1 (MI1b), which dealt primarily with intercepting transmissions and breaking codes;[9] and the Admiralty operated Room 40 (later known as NID25), which focused on interception of maritime and transatlantic communications.

It was room 40 that intercepted the famous Zimmermann Telegram: an encrypted telegram sent on January 16, 1917, by the foreign minister of Germany, Arthur Zimmerman, to the German ambassador in the United States, to be transferred to the German ambassador in Mexico, Heinrich von Eckhardt. Von Eckhardt was authorized to offer Mexico an alliance with Germany against the United States in exchange for generous financial support and an understanding of Germany on Mexico to retake the southwestern United States. The interception of the telegram by British Naval Intelligence was one of the main causes that pushed the United States to join the Principal Powers in World War I.[10]

After the war, in light of the growing popularity of means of communication, the British Cabinet's Secret Services Committee set up an agency for code breaking under the director of navy intelligence that would include the bulk of the functions of the War Office. The name of the new organization was Government Code and Cypher School and later, the Government Communications Headquarters (GCHQ), which is the name to this day.

The prevailing view is that World War II is the origin of modern intelligence, because it was the first significant event in which all intelligence efforts converged into one entity—that is, a national intelligence system. This revolution is reflected in four areas:

1. Increased collection capabilities and, in particular, the increasing dominance of signals intelligence (SIGINT) gathering, including interception of communications (COMINT) and analysis of radar-based electronic intelligence (ELINT).

2. Improvements to the organizational structures that provide decision makers with intelligence, with the lowest tier being those fighting on the battlefield. Such structures also enable intelligence organizations to cope with the abundance of information made available as a result of improvement in the means of collection.
3. Increasing development of knowledge about the intelligence profession itself and its outputs in relation to its environment (e.g., its relationship with decision makers).
4. Broadening the concept of intelligence, from a function of "observing" its surroundings to one that also involves changing its environment, such as through psychological warfare, economic warfare, and sabotage.

The Anglo-American alliance axis was at the center of this revolution, though the Soviet, Nazi (especially military), and Japanese intelligence services certainly played a role. The Brits continued to upgrade their new intelligence services and achieved impressive technological breakthroughs, notably in intercepting messages encrypted by Enigma, an encryption and decoding machine that German and Italian forces used.[11] Other technological innovations were achieved by the British forces in the area of electronic intelligence (radar signal decoding) and airplane-based visual intelligence.

Meanwhile, the Americans expanded their intelligence services and, thus, largely determined the organizational characteristics of intelligence communities around the world for the coming decades. This development had inauspicious beginnings: until the outbreak of World War II, American intelligence services lagged behind their counterparts in Europe. Isolationist decision making between the world wars led to a lack of interest in going beyond the continent. The American democratic-liberal culture did not approve of the establishment of intelligence services, which were perceived as a potential instrument by which authorities could violate individual freedoms.

This attitude is echoed several years later (1947) in the words of Senator Edward Robertson (R-WY) who opposed the establishment of a central intelligence service, saying, "The proposed agency has all the potentialities of an American Gestapo."[12] The only intelligence function that operated in a sustained and efficient manner and enjoyed resources and attention from decision makers was the FBI, which dealt with aspects of homeland security and prevention of espionage (along with other domestic threats, mainly crime).

On the eve of World War II, two small military intelligence organizations with low status had little influence on decision makers and, therefore, limited ability to produce strategic intelligence. The first was the Military Intelligence Division (MID), which was the army's intelligence body; the second was the Office of Naval Intelligence (ONI). Alongside these organizations, within the army and navy were smaller bodies that dealt with code breaking. The limited intelligence capabilities of these two bodies, as well as the problems with the then-existing intelligence arrangements (or, more precisely, the absence of arrangements), were revealed in full force at the outbreak of the war in Europe and in the continuing experience of decision makers, who were repeatedly surprised.

In July 1941, when American decision makers were still experiencing overwhelming surprise at the Nazi invasion of the Soviet Union, William Donovan was appointed head of the Office of the Coordinator of Information (CoI)—an intelligence, disinformation, and propaganda agency founded by order of President Roosevelt. That was the first major attempt to set clear boundaries for a national intelligence system, with one common goal and underlying logic.

Initially, the office's goal was to coordinate the various intelligence agencies, not an uncommon phenomenon when organizations experience growing internal complexity as a response to a growing external one. But it soon began to replicate some of their organizational functions.[13] In July 1942, the CoI was split into two: the Office of Strategic Services (OSS), which later became the Central Intelligence Agency (CIA); and the Office of War Information, which later became the U.S. Information Agency (USIA).[14] The purpose of the OSS was to carry out acts of espionage, sabotage, subversion, and propaganda in service of the American war effort.[15] As such, the OSS was subordinated to the head of the Joint Chiefs of Staff.

We cannot ignore, of course, the critical role technology had in this transformation. In World War II, intelligence entered the technological era—specifically, the field of electronic intelligence. Prior to the war, intelligence organizations around the world collected data based on electronic sources, but until the outbreak of the war, or even later, technological intelligence was not central to intelligence gathering. "Classic" methods of collection, primarily through agents, diplomats, and open sources, had dominated. Only during the war—and as the use of advanced communication means and radars became increasingly widespread—the field of signals intelligence gathering took precedence over the various other means. The development of military aviation, manifested in the mass use of attack, bombing, and cargo aircraft, along with dramatic developments in observation, photography, and analysis techniques, drove visual intelligence.

One more development came from the expansion and development of the means of collection: Processing, research, and distribution functions for intelligence materials were reactions to increasing data congestion, which, in turn, required the creation of more sophisticated mechanisms that could cope with the vast amounts of information. Subsequently, this trend led to establishment of a new field: estimative intelligence—an intelligence knowledge conveyed to national-level decision makers that constitutes the foundation for the design and management of the national strategy.[16] Estimative intelligence, organizationally expressed in the establishment of new mechanisms (such as the CIA's Directorate of Analysis, known through much of its history as the Directorate of Intelligence), relies in its essence on a broad and deep range of data collection and processing operations.

This was the crowning glory of the intelligence enterprise in the throes of revolution—a combination of traditional and new collection methods, various methodologies for knowledge development; a group of research and assessment functions that emerged as independent organizations, as well as functions within existing organizations; and a coherent logical framework to articulate intelligence work: the concept of the intelligence cycle (we will elaborate on that later). The keystone of this process was enactment of the National Security Act of 1947, which created a formal framework for the intelligence community and enabled establishment of the CIA as a professional civilian intelligence agency. To a certain extent, this development could also be seen as a reaction of the legal system to stimuli initiated by the new intelligence system.

Since its inception, this agency has been divided into two separate areas: intelligence assessment, that is, research and assessment of intelligence at the national level (Directorate of Analysis); and operational intelligence, that is, carrying out secret operations outside the United States to gather intelligence, or other activities such as sabotage, subversion, and psychological warfare (Directorate of Operations). A year later the CIA also formed the Office of Scientific Intelligence (OSI) by merging the Scientific Branch in the Office of Reports and Estimates (ORE) with the Nuclear Energy Group of the Office of Special Operation (OSO).[17]

In the 1950s, the young national intelligence establishment became a central component in American activities against the Soviet threat, especially the Soviet nuclear plan.[18] Clandestine activity became a major instrument in the various Cold War theaters. These years also witnessed what I call the "technological collection revolution"—a result of tremendous technological momentum culminating in launching a comprehensive electronic intelligence (ELINT) platform in 1954, the entry into service of the U-2 spy plane in 1956, and the reconnaissance satellite Corona System in 1960. Interestingly, these new technological developments were driven, first and foremost, by the national security establishment—a stark contradiction to our day and age, when innovation is driven primarily by the private market.

In any case, these technological developments led to a qualitative leap in American collection capabilities. For the first time, the Americans managed to define relatively precise limits to the potential Soviet nuclear threat; they also prepared an intelligence response to the so-called missile gap—the then supposed (we now know, mistaken) relative inferiority of American capabilities in development and production of ballistic missiles, specifically intercontinental ballistic missiles (ICBM).[19]

The dramatic contribution of these intelligence measures to the crystallization of the American intelligence picture of the Soviets—including measures that enabled photographic coverage beyond the Iron Curtain—demonstrated a victory for technology in the service of intelligence. They revealed that it is possible to physically overcome limitations on access to information inherent in conflict situations by technological means, a clear expression of the achievements of the national intelligence enterprise. Finally, the technological collection revolution demonstrated the need to develop research and assessment mechanisms for technological intelligence. The complexity of the technical structure of the Soviet nuclear weapons development program posed a significant challenge to American intelligence personnel; it demanded technical data that could only be obtained by new collection techniques and could only be effectively processed by analysts with specific technological expertise.[20]

This is why in 1962, the CIA formed the Deputy Directorate of Research (DDR). Under it was the newly formed Office of Special Activities, along with the Office of ELINT and the Office of Research and Development, although the OSI, Office of Scientific Intelligence, formed in 1948 by the CIA, remained part of the Directorate of Operations. In 1963, the function was renamed Deputy Directorate of Science and Technology. The OSI was transferred to the Deputy Directorate of Science and Technology, along with the Office of Computer Services. And in 1965, the Directorate was renamed again, the Directorate of Science and Technology.[21]

This technological revolution had two other important implications, which could be described as the very early signs of the intelligence system inadequacy with its changing environment: first, it encouraged simplistic approaches to national intelligence—a kind of addiction to the world of information and a Sisyphean pursuit for information that can *allegedly* clarify a vague situation; and, second, a later understanding that the entire uncertainty the Americans are facing is based on a rather solid factual basis but is spread over a broad and subjective *interpretational* space. Put differently, the wealth and breadth of new collection sensors created a false belief that the American IC could overcome any gap pertaining to American understanding of the Soviet strategy (and tactics), and that gap could be filled if only new (and more) sensors were developed and produced. Struck by the existing technological capabilities, American decision makers and intelligence practitioners ignored the fact that most strategic geopolitical challenges are a matter of sense-making rather than a gap in accessible information. This is an echo of "technological determinism"—an approach that assumes that technology holds the solution to most human issues.[22] As we shall see, some still believe in such an approach, even when it is clear that most of the past seventy years' strategic surprises haven't stemmed from lack of information but, rather, the ability to interpret the information and act on it.

The next technology-driven dramatic shift in intelligence was catalyzed by the U.S. military, especially the army and the marines, which reacted to yet another dramatic change in their environment. The conceptual shift was led by the army between 1976 and 1986, in which it developed advanced concepts, culminating in the Revolution in Military Affairs (RMA). The shift reflected a dramatic change in the perception of military intelligence, and intelligence as a whole, and it is an expression of the rare situation where two systems harmonically transform. Thus, in the 1980s, army intelligence experienced a revolution: an over-rationalization of intelligence resources and functions as the main functional domain of the military, which reflected a rise in the status of military intelligence—as expressed, for example, in a new definition of the most senior army intelligence official: from assistant chief of staff for intelligence (ACSI) to deputy chief of staff intelligence (DCSINT).[23]

At the beginning of the 1990s, with the collapse of the Soviet bloc, the U.S. Army recognized that the United States had entered a new era: the end of the Cold War and the advent of the information age. Thus, it acknowledged the need for an epistemological transformation followed by formulation of new concepts and doctrines adapted to this era. The title of one of the new field manuals published in 1993 demonstrated that nicely: "A doctrine for a New Age."[24]

The advent of the information age catalyzed another profound change in the intelligence enterprise: sensory technology, computing, and the internet all enabled a new kind of connectivity and availability of information. In American military thought, and in intelligence thinking overall, information has become a dimension, similar to air, land, sea, and space, in which it is possible to establish an advantage against adversaries. Creating such an advantage is the key to the success of national security in the information age. Thus, in August 1996, the army published a new regulation (FM 100–6) in which it expressed the adoption of the principle of information dominance, a concept that has also gained traction in the Department of Defense (DoD), which called it "information superiority."[25]

The 1991 Gulf War had profound implications for U.S. intelligence. Never had so much information been transferred so quickly from intelligence systems to combat systems with such a devastating effect. The accuracy of the weapons the United States used stunned the world, and the war emphasized the need for the armed forces to expand efforts to link intelligence systems with combat systems and to train military personnel to use these systems effectively. However, the war also exposed weaknesses in intelligence—particularly regarding the readiness for crisis in remote areas and the problematic nature of interservice coordination.

Notwithstanding that, after the American victory in the Arab/Persian Gulf and in light of the collapse of the Soviet bloc, claims arose about the need for significant cuts to the American intelligence community. As a result, the community embarked on comprehensive reforms, inspired, among other things, by the recommendations of the Gates Task Force in 1991. First, the CIA established mechanisms for the use of publicly available information and to improve CIA support for military missions. Second, and even more important, a new intelligence agency—the National Geospatial Intelligence Agency (NGA)—was established in 1996. The agency is overseen by the secretary of defense and director of national intelligence (DNI). The third reform strengthened the staff of the director of central intelligence (DCI), which supported it in its community role.

Another point of reference that illustrates the dialectic between technological development and the intelligence establishment relates to the recommendations of the Commission on the Roles and Capabilities of the U.S. Intelligence Community (Aspin-Brown Commission). The commission's mandate was to study the roles and capabilities of American intelligence agencies in the post–Cold War era and to formulate recommendations for change. The commission's report, published in 1996, recommended dramatic changes in the U.S. intelligence community. It stated that since the end of the Cold War, the allocation of resources to the community had decreased while manpower costs continued to rise, disrupting the necessary investments in new technologies and limiting functional flexibility. A series of recommendations were intended to address this problem and included ratification of the NGA under the Department of Defense and encouraging the establishment of joint intelligence centers (which will be discussed later in the book).[26]

The terrorist attacks of September 11, 2001, led to profound changes in U.S. foreign and defense policy and the organization of the national security establishment—including the American intelligence community. The report prepared by the National Commission on Terrorist Attacks upon the United States (known as the 9/11 Commission) at the request of President Bush and Congress identified the intelligence failures occurring prior to the attacks. After releasing the report, commission chair Thomas Kean declared that both presidents Clinton and Bush were "not well served" by the FBI and CIA.[27]

Indeed, some of these changes could be perceived from the technology–intelligence nexus perspective.

One of the investigation's consequences was the termination of the position of DCI and the establishment of the Office of the Director of National Intelligence (ODNI). Other changes were reflected in the form of reorganization and operations, such as establishment of the Department of Homeland

Security (DHS) and its intelligence component; as well as the creation of new intelligence components in the DoD, the Department of the Treasury, and the Drug Enforcement Administration (DEA); the organization, authorities, and activities of the counterintelligence field activity; the transformation of the Federal Bureau of Investigation's intelligence structure and activities; and changes in the U.S. interrogation and electronic surveillance policies and activities.

Additional changes were the consequence of technological and doctrinal developments: the ability to provide real-time data to military commanders led to the creation of the Joint Intelligence Operations Center (JIC) within the Defense Intelligence Agency (DIA) and the military commands. Modifications in operational activity (e.g., the targeted killings of al-Qaeda officials), were also due to technological achievements, such as the capabilities of Predator unmanned aerial vehicles to provide real-time data and the ability to mate Hellfire missiles with the Predators.

Other changes, associated with the IC's estimates of Iraq's weapons of mass destruction (WMD) programs, became the basis for the Bush administration's public information campaign in support of the decision to invade Iraq and topple Saddam Hussein. In the aftermath, the community's collection and analysis efforts became the subject of multiple investigations by the Senate Select Committee on Intelligence and other official bodies.

The "National Security Strategy 2002" added a sense of urgency to the need for a profound change in the American intelligence community, in part because of accelerating technological developments. The document emphasized the need to adapt intelligence capabilities to the new era, with an emphasis on the war on terror, and the need to shorten response times—both of which require a deeper integration of intelligence and military operations. The document, therefore, recommended strengthening the powers of the director of national intelligence, establishing a new framework for warning against terrorist events—the National Counterterrorism Center (NCTC), and developing new and advanced methods for collecting data and improving collection and processing methods.

A wide range of new offices that undertake or integrate intelligence activities has been established—yet another expression of increasing internal complexity to adequately cope with increasing external complexity. These include the Undersecretary of Defense for Intelligence, the Directorate of Information Assurance and Infrastructure Protection in the Department of Homeland Security, and the Terrorist Threat Integration Center. These developments are a logical outcome of the emphasis that U.S. intelligence has placed, since the outset of the millennium, on developing advanced intelligence capabilities and improving integration between the various agencies to ensure that the community adapts to the changing reality.[28]

Finally, another transformation, which Biltgen and Ryan refer to as the Third Age of Intelligence (the first was 1944 to 1962; the second, 1963 to 2001), emerged together with an unprecedented flood of information technologies and the proliferation of social networks. This era was focused, from a technological point of view, on the creation of an innovative mix of perspectives and deep analysis that came from a variety of intelligence sources, in other words, Multi-Int.[29] We can see this shift by examining the annual National Intelligence Strategy reports produced by the ODNI since 2005 and until 2019.

The 2005 report describes the drastic overhaul the American IC will carry out. According to this document, the IC will create a new system for sharing information while integrating its existing enterprises to meet its mission objectives and enterprise objectives. The report also included five mission objectives:

1. Defeat terrorism
2. Counter the spread of WMD
3. Support democratic, or aspiring democratic, regimes
4. Improve the community's analytic capabilities (with a special emphasis on improving human intelligence, HUMINT, collection)
5. Increase the role of strategic forecasting, or predictive intelligence

Of the seven enterprise objectives the report included, two focused on technology: optimize collection capabilities, including an increase in collection from open sources, human sources, and better use of technology among the entire intelligence community; and establish a uniform process for scientific and technological activities, requiring that new trends in technological advancement be identified by "establishing a centrally led, but de-centrally executed, process" within the intelligence community.

In 2009, six mission objectives were defined in the following order:

1. Radical violent warfare
2. Weapons of mass destruction, held by governmental and nongovernmental actors
3. The provision of strategic intelligence and early warning for policy makers
4. Counterespionage
5. Improved cyber security to protect U.S. information infrastructures
6. Support for military operations[30]

By contrast, the 2014 and 2019 reports defined seven mission objectives. The first four relate to the basic tasks of the intelligence community, whereas the other three relate to thematic domains:

1. Strategic intelligence—issues relating to the U.S. national security interest
2. Intelligence to support forecasting and early warning
3. Operational support
4. Cyber threats posed by governmental and nongovernmental actors
5. Terrorism
6. The challenge and risk of WMD by governmental and nongovernmental actors
7. Counterespionage[31]

These changes demonstrate how technological shifts have catalyzed changes in the IC's mission: the most notable change is the growing importance of the IC in what Moore and others call sense-making: the need to support decision makers with relevant and actionable strategic intelligence, and develop forecasting, prediction, and early warning mechanisms to inform decision makers about changes in the strategic environment.[32] These two changes (the latter not included in the 2009 document) demonstrate the decision makers' (and consequently, the IC's) need for sense-making in a rapidly changing environment, where information is abundant but actionable insights are by far more challenging to produce.

The basic structure of the agencies also evolved. In 2005, Congress passed a law establishing the position of director of national intelligence. The DNI is the leader of the U.S. intelligence community and is prohibited from serving as the CIA director or the head of any other intelligence community element at the same time. In addition, the law required the CIA director to report his agency's activities to the DNI.

Another notable structural change, directly linked to technological changes, is the establishment of the director of national intelligence Open Source Center (OSC). This is a CIA intelligence center providing analysis of open-source intelligence materials. Established in November 2005, by the Office of the Director of National Intelligence, OSC is tasked with improving the availability of open sources to intelligence officers and other government officials. Another organization established around that time was the Intelligence Advanced Research Projects Activity (IARPA). Authorized by the ODNI in 2006, IARPA was modeled after the U.S. Defense Advanced Research Projects Agency (DARPA) but focused on national intelligence needs rather than military needs. The agency was a consolidation of the National Security Agency's Disruptive Technology Office, the National

Geospatial-Intelligence Agency's National Technology Alliance, and the Central Intelligence Agency's Intelligence Technology Innovation Center.

Finally, within the CIA, in 2015, as part of a change in its organizational structure (in which ten central and geographic mission centers were established), a new fifth directorate was established for the first time in fifty years: the Directorate of Digital Innovation (DDI). According to the CIA's website, the DDI is

> focused on accelerating innovation across the Agency's mission activities with cutting-edge digital and cyber tradecraft and IT infrastructure. The DDI is the engine of creativity, integration, and rigor that CIA needs in the digital age, ensuring that our culture, tradecraft, and knowledge management across the board are more than equal to the challenges and opportunities of the rapidly changing world in which we operate. From arming our officers with the tools and techniques they need to excel and prevail in the cyber and big data arenas to optimizing our business operations, the DDI is a strong, agile partner with the other Directorates, our Mission Centers, and our Intelligence Community counterparts to deliver the insights our nation requires.[33]

Another aspect of the American IC's reaction to the changing technological environment pertains to the emergence of cyberspace as a unique domain, similar to air, space, land, and sea. The IC's reaction could be divided into three historical phases; each adheres to the changing nature of the cyber domain itself, and each represents a reaction to a meaningful event in which the community was surprised by a certain type of adversarial cyber-attack.[34]

The first period was the forming years, while the internet was in its infancy. Indeed, the first meaningful attack on U.S. digital infrastructure took place in 1986—an event dubbed Cuckoo's Egg in which the KGB was involved in an invasion of the networks of Lawrence Berkeley Lab. However, the first significant cyber-attack is considered to be the Morris worm or Internet worm of November 2, 1988, one of the first computer worms distributed via the internet and the first to gain significant mainstream media attention. A computer worm is a type of malware that spreads copies of itself from computer to computer. The Morris worm was written by a graduate student at Cornell University, Robert Tappan Morris, and launched on November 2, 1988, from the computer systems of the Massachusetts Institute of Technology as an experiment. It caused the collapse of some six thousand computers (then, about 10 percent of the global internet).

The event revealed how vulnerable the national digital infrastructure was and demonstrated the need to create proper mechanisms to secure the national cyber-domain. Following the event, in 1988 DARPA founded, at Carnegie Mellon University, CERT—coordination center of the computer emergency response team. CERT partnered with government, industry, law enforcement, and academia to develop advanced methods and technologies to counter large-scale, sophisticated cyber threats. In the following years, the Congress initiated legislation aimed at securing privacy in the digital space.[35]

The second stage started with the "Moonlight Maze" incident in 1999, considered to be one of the first widely known cyber espionage campaigns in history. In 1999 the U.S. government investigated a massive data breach of classified information. It started in 1996 and affected NASA, the Pentagon, military contractors, civilian academics, the Department of Energy, and numerous other American government agencies. The Russian government was blamed for the attacks, although initially little evidence backed up the U.S. accusations besides a Russian IP address that was traced to the hack. Nevertheless, the well-orchestrated attack demonstrated the involvement of foreign governments in sophisticated cyber-attacks, as well as the vulnerability of the information domain—where adversaries could obtain access to sensitive information. Further, the event demonstrated the key differences between visible kinetic attacks, where adversaries are known; and cyber-attacks, where the attackers, the targets, and the potential damage are somewhat unknown.

Following that new understanding, the U.S. government undertook several important steps: the Presidential Decision Directive (PDD-63) called for a range of actions intended to improve federal agency security programs, improve the nation's ability to detect and respond to serious computer-based and physical attacks, and establish a partnership between the government and the private sector.

To achieve these goals, PDD-63 established and designated organizations to provide central coordination and support, such as the National Coordinator for Security, Infrastructure Protection, and Counter-Terrorism; the Critical Infrastructure Assurance Office (CIAO); and the National Infrastructure Assurance Council (NIAC). Two organizations were important in the context of intelligence work: first, the National Infrastructure Protection Center (NIPC) at the FBI, which involves representatives from the bureau, the Department of Defense, the Secret Service, the intelligence community, and several other departments, as well as the private sector, in an information sharing and collaboration effort. NIPC also provided the principal means of facilitating and coordinating the federal response to an incident, mitigating attacks, investigating threats, and monitoring reconstitution efforts. Second was the Joint Task Force-Global Network Operations (JTF-GNO), a subordinate command of the U.S. Strategic Command whose mission was to direct the operation and defense of the Global Information Grid (GIG) across strategic, operational, and tactical boundaries in support of the U.S. Department of Defense's full spectrum of war fighting, intelligence, and business operations.

The third phase followed the Stuxnet attack. Stuxnet was a malicious computer worm first uncovered in 2010 and thought to have been in development since at least 2005. Stuxnet targets supervisory control and data acquisition (SCADA) systems and is believed to be responsible for causing substantial damage to the nuclear program of Iran. Although neither country has openly admitted responsibility, the worm is widely understood to be a cyber-weapon built jointly by the United States and Israel in a collaborative effort known as the "Olympic Games."[36]

The case demonstrated the difficulties in identifying cyber-attacks as well as the understanding that national level attacks are difficult to identify. The revelation prompted a series of activities at the multinational level including a cyber agreement between the United States and China (2015).

Looking more broadly, the U.S. IC bears the responsibility for tackling most of modern cyber warfare activities. In terms of cyber defense, the IC focuses on three important aspects: organization, detection, and deterrence. For example, the ODNI leads the efforts to identify potential cyber-attacks; the DHS leads the infrastructure security efforts; the DoD plans strategies to cyber counterattacks; the NSA monitors, identifies, reports, and responds to cyber threats; and the FBI is in charge of investigation and prosecution of cyber-crime initiators. Outside of the IC are several other organizations, most prominently the U.S. Cyber Command (USCYBERCOM); created in mid-2009, it cooperates with NSA networks and since its inception has been headed concurrently by the director of the National Security Agency. Although originally created with a defensive mission in mind, it has increasingly been viewed as an offensive force.[37]

It is worth mentioning several dramatic changes that other intelligence communities have experienced in the past decade—most closely associated with the advent of new technologies. In Britain, the National Security Council (NSC) was established in 2010 to improve and formalize the links between the intelligence community and decision makers, which previously had been carried out in informal groups of officials. The NSC is in charge of presenting the British National Security Strategy, which includes intelligence prioritization, as determined by the Joint Intelligence Committee (JIC), primarily for the MI6 and the GCHQ.[38] Similar to the American case, both demonstrate the need for a centralized control over the intelligence community at the national level. In both cases, the changes that occurred on the structures of these ICs reflect the gap between the *idea* of centralized control and its manifestation. In the American case, the 9/11 attacks created the conditions needed for "unification" of the IC under a new governing entity (the DNI); in the British case, the chase was much more modest though persistent.

Another reaction to the technological aspect of the changing environment pertains to the emergence of the cyber domain. In 2014, the GCHQ and the

Minisrty of Defence created the National Offensive Cyber Program, responsible for developing and operating offensive cyber capabilities.[39] In 2016 a new function was established in the GCHQ: National Cyber Security Centre (NCSC), which deals with cyber defense, including advising and supporting the public and private sector in how to avoid computer security threats, and devising a cyber security strategy for the United Kingdom.

Although these initiatives don't reflect a radical transformation of the British IC, the National Security Capability Review from 2018 does emphasize the need for innovation, especially in fields related to science and technology, as well as data collection and analysis.[40] One can hope that such understandings will be translated into a major transformation rather than local adjustments.

In Australia, following an intelligence review published in 2017, the Office of National Assessments (ONA) was expanded to the Office of National Intelligence (ONI), a change that reflects establishment of an organization in charge of coordinating the Australian IC.[41] Another change directly linked to technological transformation is the transition of the Australian Signals Directorate (ASD) to an independent agency rather than an organization nested under the DoD. As such, the ASD is also in charge of cyber security.[42]

In both cases, the U.S. and British communities identified the need to create a more integrated structure, one that would allow for systemic integration in a given operational context (e.g., "war on terror"). But unlike the American case, which focused on creating new organizational functions, the Brits focused on better and more efficient use of existing resources and promoting less formal cross-organizational mechanisms for collaboration. In any case, and despite certain differences (the dramatic changes in the American case, less so in the British one), the driving forces leading to changes are similar: changes in the nature of the threats these countries face, advances in both military and intelligence doctrines in light of emerging technologies—all require structural and operational coordination of the intelligence community, and drive for greater integration at the national, strategic, operational, and tactical levels.

However, as we shall later discuss, despite these organizational changes, intelligence agencies have taken modest efforts to overhaul their basic processes. They still rely on the intelligence cycle and other practices that assume a fairly static, limited supply of knowledge. In chapter 3, we'll discuss the debate over a deep-seated transformation to reflect the full potential of digital technologies.

Chapter 2

New and Emerging Threats

Given the changing nature of the threats, the collapse of the Soviet Union and the Communist bloc led to a dramatic change in the nature and scope of intelligence missions. Compared to the Cold War, during which intelligence agencies faced one major defined threat, the new world was characterized by a lack of focus, alongside a multitude of challenges and tasks facing intelligence communities. Local conflicts, climatic issues, epidemic outbreaks, the connection between crime and terrorism, and the need to protect human rights are just some of the threats that intelligence organizations have had to—and still have to—deal with.

Emerging technologies pose new threats to intelligence organizations and give new meaning to existing threats, mainly because their adversaries also use them and will continue to do so. Advanced technological capabilities may enable enemies and adversaries to detect, disrupt, negate, and defraud Western intelligence efforts. Further, as the technological arms race intensifies, the battlefield will expand to new dimensions in which intelligence organizations are at a disadvantage. This disadvantage stems from the role of intelligence organizations in democratic regimes, the structure and organization of intelligence communities as part of the national security enterprise, and how intelligence organizations are built and operated. In contrast, adversaries such as China and Russia suffer less from these limitations, mainly due to the legal and structural blurring between the public and private spheres and the amorphous nature of the legal environment in which these organizations operate—two aspects that democratic regimes consider sacred.[1]

Moreover, the same advanced technologies also improve the adversaries' defense capabilities against the West's intelligence operations. For example, quantum computing, in which China is considered a pioneer, will dramatically upgrade its cyber defense capabilities. It will also improve China's ability to operate human agents in a sensor-saturated environment where all activity, human and otherwise, is frequently monitored. Indeed, these resources will also dramatically improve cyber-attack capabilities, but experience teaches us that in the cat-and-mouse intelligence-technology game, it is easier to develop more advanced defensive capabilities than to develop improved offensive capabilities. The latter will come, but belatedly, which would lead to intelligence blindness. This blindness, even if temporary, could spur strategic problems for democratic regimes, as evidenced by the current challenges to cope with considerable disinformation efforts.

This study does not purport to map the range of current and future threats, focusing only on those directly related to the technologies examined here. But it is clear that there are some challenges in distinguishing between direct and indirect connections to technology and types of threats. It is also clear that threats are always context-dependent, and that what one nation may define as a threat, another may define as an opportunity. Thus, over the following pages, I will present a bird's-eye view of the main threats that intelligence organizations face or will face in Western countries, and, as usual, I will focus on threats that are mainly relevant to democratic regimes. I will focus on emerging threats (i.e., threats that are considered relatively new), not those that are well-known to ICs, such as terrorism or the proliferation of unconventional weapons. Hence, the threats reviewed here meet two main criteria:

1. First, these are relatively new threats, or at least threats that hitherto have not been at the core of Western intelligence activities.
2. Second, these threats will not be dealt with through existing organizational structures, operating concepts, or capabilities; rather, they will require ICs to expand their expertise and responsibilities, establish dedicated bodies, and develop new intelligence capabilities.

The following pages focus on the threats that exist in the external organizational environment for intelligence communities, not the internal environment. Threats and challenges of the latter type are mentioned in chapter 3.

The threats reviewed here have one thing in common, which is that they blur traditional boundaries: they are global in the sense that they cross nation-state borders and traverse the traditional division between threats related to national security and homeland security, or simply between defense and security. The former usually refers to military defense against threats from state adversaries or those acting on their behalf; the latter refers to dealing with and recovering from threats directed at civilians, mainly by terrorist and criminal bodies, or as a result of natural disasters and other emergencies.

Three main threats are directly related to emergence of the new technologies referred to above:

1. The use of technologies to affect the hearts and minds of individuals and groups.

2. The danger of falling behind in the scientific-technological arms race.
3. Threats to human security as manifested in climatic dangers and epidemic outbreaks.

THE STRUGGLE OVER PUBLIC CONSCIOUSNESS

In September 2020, the FBI and NCSC (National Counterintelligence and Security Center) released a half-hour feature film called *The Nevernight Connection*, which describes how Chinese intelligence services use social networks as a tool to spread misinformation and to obtain classified information. In the film, we see an ex-member of a technological unit in the U.S. Navy arrive in China at the invitation of a fictitious research institute and slowly realize that he has been duped. The film is based on a true story. It was first distributed to the U.S. IC to give intelligence personnel tools to identify such operations. Later, it was released for public viewing "to raise awareness among Americans so they can guard against online approaches from unknown parties that could put them, their organization and even national security at risk."[2]

The main threat, which to a large extent is also relevant to the other two threats discussed in this chapter, is the use of information technology to influence the hearts and minds of individuals and groups. This is, in fact, a new type of combat—one that is not kinetic (i.e., does not involve live fire and does not cause visible losses). True, such influence (i.e., psychological warfare) can occur in armed conflicts in which kinetic power is activated. However, the destructive potential of this threat lies precisely in its elusive nature and its ability to both directly and indirectly influence the results of conflicts between democratic regimes and their adversaries.[3] This threat is particularly valid in light of the fact that the main rivals of Western countries, led by China, Russia, and to some extent Iran, make sophisticated use of technological means to shape the social consciousness to gain ground, sometimes without the use of direct force (i.e., kinetic force).

Endeavors to impact public consciousness, which include dissemination of disinformation, are probably the most significant challenge facing intelligence services into the foreseeable future. We already are seeing an unprecedented leap—not only in the technological capabilities themselves, but also in the use that various parties are making of them. Technologies such as generative adversarial network (GAN), or generative neural network architectures in general, enable what is known as deepfake or synthetic media—high-level manipulation of video or audio content that cannot be distinguished from the real thing. The challenge for intelligence agencies is twofold:

1. To the ocean of "real" information with which organizations must contend is added another layer of information that requires processing.
2. Intelligence agencies must also locate false information within the broad information ocean—a highly complex challenge.

The most obvious manifestation of threats to social consciousness is foreign influence on democratic processes. Indeed, this is not a new threat: it was common during the Cold War. But in recent years—and especially in light of Russian interference in the 2016 U.S. presidential election and other attempts to influence European elections—it appears to be the most significant threat to democracies. This threat has the potential not only to disrupt democratic processes such as free elections, but also to undermine the foundations of the democratic regime itself. Thus, it is a strategic threat of the highest order.

For the most part, world superpowers are behind such destabilizing actions. In operating covert campaigns to affect the public's consciousness, their purpose is to influence public discourse; promote narratives that serve them (the campaign initiator); sow confusion, chaos, and mistrust; and undermine the basic social contract at the core of democratic regimes. Such actions may be manifested in many dimensions that are not purely political, including the economy, culture, education, and the media. The means of carrying out the campaigns are also varied and may be direct—including through financial assistance, diplomacy, or publicly conveying messages—but they may also be covert and indirect. These campaigns also make use of emerging technologies related to the dominance of social networks in human culture. Technological tools enable the campaign initiator to reach broad and diverse target audiences, to target specific audiences, and to tailor specific messages to them—both true and false.

Mika Aaltola, director of the Finnish Institute for International Affairs, put forward four examples of foreign interference in public discourse, particularly in elections in democratic regimes:

1. The use of disinformation to stoke rifts and tensions. Foreign disinformation campaigns provide a convenient infrastructure for election intervention, and their purpose usually is to create polarization and distrust in the democratic system. These campaigns are especially effective when carried out through social media.
2. The theft of sensitive information. The purpose of this type of action is to advance certain candidates over others; to create public scandals by leaking sensitive information; or even to publish the fact that sensitive information has been revealed, as evidenced in the 2016 U.S. presidential election.

3. Conveying sensitive or false information that originated on social media through traditional media.
4. Conspiracy with a candidate or party in exchange for political or other recompense.

Indeed, Western intelligence communities are increasingly required to address this challenge, and it is reasonable to assume that they do not refrain from carrying out similar operations of their own. The characteristics of the threat, which include covert state involvement across a variety of communication channels, particularly digital, make intelligence organizations particularly suited to tackling the challenge. Of particular note in this regard are the report that the American intelligence community published after the 2016 presidential election; the comprehensive intelligence assessments leading up to the 2020 elections; and the report by the Intelligence Committee of the British Parliament, which pointed out significant failures of the British community in the face of this challenge. However, other intelligence communities, including the Israeli one, opt to exclude themselves from addressing this threat—at least publicly—both because they are more comfortable dealing with traditional threats (such as terrorism) and because of the political repercussions of addressing the issue. After all, it is difficult to distinguish between external and internal influences on democratic processes, and sometimes the very preoccupation with the issue paints intelligence organizations as supporters of one side of the political map at the expense of the other.

THE TECHNOLOGICAL ARMS RACE

A second threat concerns the need to gain an advantage in the technological arms race. One of the central issues at the core of superpower relations at present is gaining technological supremacy, or at least dominance, as a fundamental component of national security policy. Cyber supremacy, artificial intelligence, or even quantum supremacy have all been mentioned in recent years as strategic overarching goals of the superpowers and smaller states alike.

Since 2014, the leaders of several countries, including of the world's leading superpowers in terms of technology and economics, have valued the importance of advanced technologies, such as AI or quantum computing, to the power of the countries they lead. China, the United States, Russia, some EU countries, and even Israel, for example, have already built national programs in these areas and are allocating massive resources and attention to them to push their countries forward. Most strategies in this vein emphasize the importance of technological developments as an engine of economic growth and, further, for national security, including military applications.

Indeed, from the outset, the struggle between superpowers has been characterized by attempts to achieve technological advantage—prominent examples include achieving nuclear capabilities, command of the sea, and the race to space. Achieving such an advantage has always hinged on the ability to obtain and use information and knowledge. But what distinguishes the current era is the volume and availability of useful information and the ability to make use of it. Moreover, although obtaining scientific and technological intelligence has long been a task assigned to Western intelligence services, it is still not a top priority compared to other, much more concrete and immediate threats, such as terrorism. Now, to achieve scientific advantage, intelligence organizations will have to prioritize the issue and develop capabilities for understanding and predicting technological developments and their implications for national security in its broadest sense.

Among Western countries, dissatisfaction is growing with their position in relation to their main competitors, primarily Russia and China. Many express dissatisfaction with the standing of the United States in the race for the development of innovative technologies. Gaining a leading position and continued advantage in the development of a variety of technologies now seen as groundbreaking is perceived as critical to the national security of the United States and to maintaining its status as a leading world power. However, it is clear that in some of the technologies, China currently enjoys a leading position.[4]

As in the issue of the struggle over public consciousness, the disadvantage the West faces in the technological arms race, particularly in relation to China, is partly due to China's centralized management and the fact that the government, in addition to controlling all public agencies, largely controls the private sector. In addition, China holds inexhaustible databases on its own population, the collection of which is made possible thanks to the authorities' disregard for human rights, including the right to privacy. However, for the very same reasons, China is experiencing difficulties recruiting experts, who hold fears about the theft of intellectual property and the moral consequences of the authorities' use of the technology they will develop.

The technological arms race has long-term, far-reaching effects and is already reshaping the international arena. Current and potential effects include risks related to the safety of the various applications of new technologies; effects on the arms—including nuclear weapons—that various countries may develop; conflict escalation; wider disparities between developed and developing countries, and in general; and reshaping of power dynamics in the international arena. In addition to these concerns, international law is currently unable to regulate the use and distribution of new technologies, especially in military and security contexts. The role of ICs in monitoring and predicting technological developments is therefore clear.

THE GROWING THREATS TO HUMAN SECURITY

"Climate change is an existential threat to the planet and is also dramatically affecting the national security threat landscape facing the country. Its impacts must be the subject of intense and sustained focus by the Intelligence Community."[5] These remarks were made in early 2021 by the chairman of the U.S. House Permanent Select Committee on Intelligence, Adam Schiff, following President Biden's request for a national intelligence assessment on climate change. The president's request represents a new understanding among Western decision makers that climate change has significant implications for national security.

Until just a few years ago, climate and environmental issues were considered best left to experts or climate enthusiasts. Despite international conventions, such as the Paris Agreement of 2016, it appeared that most world governments, especially the most industrialized and polluting countries, did not necessarily link these issues to national security. The four years of Donald Trump's presidency, during which, among other things, he withdrew the United States from the Paris Agreement, reversed the progress already made in the realms of climate and the environment, and damaged international cooperation efforts. Even worse, former president Trump's decision led to the exclusion of these issues from the national security discourse. His disregard for science and the authority of experts, his promotion of conspiracy theories, or simply his spreading of climate change denial lies contributed to pushing the issue off the National Security Enterprise agenda.

The COVID-19 crisis that struck the entire world has led to an important shift in perception, as countries and leaders have realized the lateral and systemic impact of such crises on the functioning of states. The epidemic has brought the debate on climatic and environmental issues back to the global agenda. The crisis has demonstrated not only how matters of health can cause a global crisis with dire consequences, but also how the steps each of us take have far-reaching implications for present and future generations. The epidemic even prominently illustrated that the patterns of behavior we take for granted today can and should change in light of new circumstances. And last, the scientific advancement and mobilization of scientists from around the world to address the coronavirus, have demonstrated not only the power of science, but also the potential inherent in global technological collaboration.[6]

A national security threat is defined as a onetime or ongoing event, the occurrence of which will seriously impair the security of the state's population and basic welfare; the state's ability to function routinely over time; its sovereignty; its strategic assets; or its ability to realize its basic national goals. Threats to national security, therefore, are not limited to military and political risks, but also include epidemics; natural disasters; exceptional climatic events; man-made disasters, such as the 1986 Chernobyl disaster; severe social and economic crises; and any combination of the above.[7] It is no wonder, then, that issues related to human security become dominant on the national security establishment's agenda. Reference to natural disasters, including epidemics, as risks to national security appears in various countries' national security strategy documents, including those of the United States and Britain.[8]

Nevertheless, although national and local government bodies have recently been involved in attempts to better understand the threats that climatic and environmental issues pose to national security, the intelligence services of most Western countries still lack dedicated bodies engaged in the field. It seems that even on this matter, ICs operate under an outdated paradigm—one that sees national security threats only as those that emerge from a lethal, powerful, and relatively short-term event, such as a terrorist attack or war, that end and are followed by recovery.

But the new realm of threats embodies a different kind of logic that ICs are not prepared for: deadly events—such as epidemics that could last for years; or a crisis caused by a change in humanity's basic conditions, such as the anticipated climate change, which will no doubt last for decades, and it is doubtful whether it will be possible to repair the damage caused. These two types of crises (epidemics and climate change) embody potential damage to an extent that we have not yet known, far beyond the state level. They suggest plausible scenarios in which humanity will have to live in crisis conditions over an extended period while defending itself or adapting to new conditions. Awareness of and vigilance against such types of threats should affect preparations for their occurrence and how they are managed from the moment they occur: as the COVID-19 crisis has shown, a large disparity will be likely between the reference scenario and its actual realization. Early assessments and preparation for a variety of scenarios, even if partial, can be the difference between life and death on a global scale, and intelligence organizations must play a key role in equipping decision makers with the knowledge they need.

Chapter 3

The Challenge to Intelligence Organizations

The intelligence cycle has long been at the heart of how Western intelligence agencies are structured and work. It rests on a few major assumptions: National security is threatened by well-defined, discrete threats, posed primarily by large nation-states. The more information policy makers have on these political-military threats (and the economies that support them), the better they can defend the nation. Most of this information is secret or hidden and can be obtained only with large investments in technological and human resources. The agency's job is to marshal those resources to gather as many pieces of information as possible (collection); process them to generate knowledge (analysis); and disseminate that knowledge to policy makers, the agencies' clients, and the consumers of intelligence deliverables. To fill the inevitable gaps in information, agencies need greater budgets to expand their sensors, as well as better processes and methodologies for collection and analysis.

Those assumptions worked fairly well for Western agencies in the Cold War. Even the collapse of the Soviet bloc and the 2001 terrorist attacks, which broadened the number of major threats, left the logic of the intelligence cycle largely intact. But since then, the landscape for national security has changed radically. New and emerging technologies have upset all of the assumptions behind the intelligence cycle. To remain relevant to policy makers, intelligence agencies must transform their missions, structures, and processes.

Leaders and scholars on intelligence are coming around to the need for transformation. Just how the agencies should transform themselves, however, is hotly debated.

THE DEBATE ABOUT TRANSFORMATION

Since World War II, the landscape for national security has continually evolved, and writings on intelligence have responded accordingly. Led by Sherman Kent, researchers into the 1970s analyzed past intelligence surprises and urged reforms to better secure the nation.[1] Improvements in espionage received the most attention during the height of the Cold War, in both academic and popular accounts. Researchers also offered comparative analyses of the Western and Soviet intelligence establishment.[2] After the 2001 attacks and the mistaken findings on weapons in Iraq, the literature focused on organizational reforms in the intelligence establishment. Particularly important were reducing the politicization of intelligence and improving the dynamics between intelligence officers and decision makers. The fight against global terrorist organizations puts the spotlight on the IC's role in this effort.[3]

Some researchers at this time suggested deeper reforms. For example, in 2005, Georgetown University Press published *Transforming U.S. Intelligence*, a collection of essays urging changes to the art and practice of intelligence, not just its bureaucratic arrangements. Most of the authors argued for overhauling policies and practices to tackle future challenges to U.S. security. But their specific recommendations were not so dramatic, as most of these were limited to one discipline or aspect of intelligence work.[4]

The first deep investigation into the future of intelligence took place a year later with RAND's "Revolution in Intelligence Affairs" workshop. This work involved intelligence leaders as well as academics. It incorporated emerging digital technologies and assessed the need for transformation in intelligence structures and operations.[5] The workshop's publications attracted little attention at first, as radical technological innovations related to intelligence were still in their infancy. Most intelligence personnel, especially at the leadership levels, had grown up before 1990 and lacked an intuitive feel for these advances. They were educated and trained at the peak of the Cold War, when the intelligence cycle, with all of its explicit and implicit assumptions, dominated. Big data and AI were not widely accessible, nor was digital fakery widespread. These and other digital technologies had to reach a level of maturity for leaders to realize their potential.

The Arab Spring of 2011 was a turning point. Not only did it catch intelligence organizations by surprise, but it showed the new digital technologies empowering ordinary people. It also showed that the methods of intelligence organizations were ill-suited to meet the challenges that these technologies catalyzed. Consequently, new studies offered new methodologies for data collection, intelligence analysis, predictions, and forecasting.[6]

Since then, scores of publications, academic and nonacademic, have called for intelligence changes as part of a broad transformation of the national security establishment.[7] When it comes to details, however, most of these seemingly bold pronouncements still call for evolutionary rather than revolutionary change. They leave the basic "industrial model" centered on the intelligence cycle and just add or change certain existing components. Some call for better tradecraft or suggest new methodologies for intelligence analysis. Others promote new concepts such as cultural and political intelligence and even intelligence for protecting personal information.[8]

One reason for their conservatism is that they focus on geopolitical threats, especially military and terrorist ones. They justify transformation on the wider threat environment, not technological change per se. They start with the familiar threats, from nuclear proliferation to terrorist groups and the failing states that often spawn them. They note that terrorists have now expanded to cyberspace, and we have lone wolves, or "super empowered digital angry men," to paraphrase Thomas Friedman's term.[9] To these they add the old new threats from superpower nations, especially newly ambitious Russia and ascendant China, with theaters extending into Earth's orbit and cyberspace. Regional powers such as Iran and North Korea are also of concern. Besides military attacks, these states could hack economic and physical infrastructure and compromise elections.

They also cite emerging threats beyond the political-military arena, such as climate change, epidemics, and the migrations that often result from these and other forces. These issues are becoming more prominent in official publications by governments and organizations around the industrialized world, and to a lesser extent, when discussing the need for such transformation.[10]

By focusing on the threat environment, rather than how digital technologies are changing the operating environment, reformers end up calling for only modest changes. They usually advise agencies to cover these added threats with new technologies, better analytic techniques, and limited structural adjustments. They say little about the basic definition, mission, and function of intelligence, as well as intelligence's new role in national security.

A few observers, however, in the past few years, have called for deep-seated changes, and their calls are now taking on new saliency.[11] These observers are aware of the growing performance and anticipated gaps between how intelligence organizations are built and operate and what is needed—and will be needed—from them in the future. In 2011, building on the work at RAND, William Lahneman wrote *Keeping U.S. Intelligence Effective: The Need for a Revolution in Intelligence Affairs*.[12] It is worth discussing his work at length, as he did more than call for going beyond the Cold War fixation on superpowers and client states. His arguments also reveal the shortcomings of the current thinking about the tectonic shifts required in intelligence work.

Lahneman argued that the fall of the Soviet Union had altered the nature and scope of intelligence work but not the paradigm under which agencies operated. The post–9/11 reforms had given the intelligence community an integrated overarching structure but left unchanged the underlying structures and processes. He called for a new intelligence paradigm fitted to both the new military threats and emerging digital technologies.

This new paradigm, he wrote, was essential for Western agencies to carry out their mission. The Soviet collapse had shifted intelligence work from a single dominant threat to a variety of new threats, yet agencies were dealing with sharply lower budgets. He quoted James Woolsey, President Clinton's CIA director, saying it was easier for the IC to supervise the USSR than to investigate the numerous threats that emerged after the Cold War. The mismatch created tension between the intelligence community and decision makers and prevented consensus on the key intelligence challenges and on the consumers of intelligence.

Lahneman called for a broader concept of relevant knowledge in intelligence. He also sought greater data sharing and collaboration within agencies and on the outside, with universities and the private sector. He sought wider recruiting and meaningful changes in intelligence training, along with a new paradigm of intelligence, one that includes a deep change in the community's missions and values, as well as structural and methodological changes.

Yet even his new paradigm was only a partial advance. He believed that the intelligence establishment should continue to maintain, in the face of some threats, the established paradigm. The traditional roles of providing early warnings of attacks on U.S. interests and giving decision makers relevant and actionable knowledge should remain intact. And although he discusses the "age of information," he says little about digital advances that created collaborative tools and spaces for national security organizations. His willingness to have the new paradigm coexist with the old one made his vision untenable.

Fully implemented, his new approach would only flood intelligence organizations with information without changing how they work with this information. The burden on one of the most challenged functions of intelligence, research and analysis, would only increase. The result would be a growing disconnect between expanded collections, overwhelmed analysts, and decision makers struggling with outdated, convoluted intelligence products.

Another important book was *Sensemaking: A Structure for an Intelligence Revolution*, by David Moore, also in 2011.[13] He likewise called for a paradigmatic shift in intelligence, but he went deeper than Lahneman in attacking the intelligence cycle itself as outdated. Agencies now faced what Horst Rittel called "wicked problems"—those that are difficult to solve because of incomplete, contradictory, and changing requirements.[14] Agencies, Moore argued, could not address these problems with just expanded collection capabilities and improved tradecraft. He urged agencies to focus on sense-making, not providing discrete knowledge, to help decision makers address these problems.

Like Lahneman, however, Moore paid little attention to emerging technologies. Even academic observers who went so far as to see cyberattacks as the main threat, and the cyber domain as the new theater, missed the political, social, economic, and cultural ramifications of this technological revolution.

One more book worth mentioning is *The Future of Intelligence*. Published by Routledge in 2015, this collection of articles includes several calls for a radical transformation, along with pessimism about "the ability of the intelligence community to function as a learning, adaptive institution."[15] Although several articles in this book present radical new concepts, the book as a whole doesn't present a comprehensive framework for such transformation.

Intelligence community leaders, however, have incorporated digital developments into their calls for transformation. Recent articles and talks by current and former intelligence executives have focused on technology-driven transformation and offered new concepts, definitions, and missions for intelligence organizations. They represent a growing perceived gap (i.e., the understanding of discrepancies between what is required from ICs in this day and age, and how they are set to meet those expectations).

Here are a few interesting examples.

Earlier in 2019, Ellen McCarthy, assistant secretary of state for the U.S. Bureau of Intelligence and Research (INR), pointed out two major shortcomings in the intelligence community: delays in introducing new technologies and difficulties in quickly and efficiently harnessing open-source intelligence. By contrast, she added, the private sector excels in both areas.[16]

Christopher Scolese, director of the National Reconnaissance Office (NRO), which buys and develops America's intelligence satellites, made a similar point in his testimony for confirmation the same year. He said his agency's biggest challenges were staying ahead of adversaries with new technology without disrupting current operations and increasing the speed of handling data without compromising its integrity and reliability.[17]

John Sherman, chief information officer of the U.S. intelligence community, noted in 2020, "Our adversaries are moving out quickly, in many areas, such as cyber, AI, machine learning, information and asymmetric warfare, not to mention other capabilities such as conventional arms and space." He added that this arena is increasingly defined by technology, data, and security, and prevailing here will require greater innovation and partnership with industry, academia, and allies.[18]

Even before that, former director of national intelligence Dan Coats argued in 2018 that the U.S. intelligence community needs to be much more innovative, agile, and flexible. He called for a revolution in intelligence work to promote the rapid adoption of new technologies; new concepts for information, knowledge, and infrastructure management; and wider and deeper collaboration with the private sector.[19] Former CIA director Mike Pompeo has similarly argued for greater agility and adaptiveness to constant change.[20]

Also in 2019, Glenn Gerstell, general counsel at the National Security Agency, justified transformation because technology is now advancing faster than society and governments can adjust to it; big data analytics are challenging our norms on privacy; cyberwarfare is becoming practical even for nonstate malefactors; and enemies are using the internet to undermine democracy. Gerstell called for a heavy government investment in intelligence so agencies could quickly adopt technologies and attract the talent to best use them. He also called for intelligence agencies to collaborate much more with the private sector.[21] Similar arguments were presented by the former acting director of the Central Intelligence Agency, Michael Morell, and Amy Zegart, an American academic.[22]

Why Digital Technology Is Different

Chapter 1 explains that technology and intelligence have always gone hand in hand: technology changed intelligence, and intelligence organizations developed new technologies that later became widespread. But this age is different, as the key technologies now are exponential: they are improving so quickly, becoming so inexpensive, and creating so many diverse applications that agencies need to approach them differently. They are shaping major industries and all aspects of our lives.

This chapter, and this book, focuses on the following technologies:

- Big data, Internet of Things (IoT), and 5G: We can now collect and analyze unprecedented amounts of information, flowing from practically almost any device or appliance.
- Advanced storage technologies: We can now store, and make readily available, enormous quantities of data at a fairly low price.
- AI and robotics: Machines can now find patterns in a blizzard of data, thanks to rapid advances in computing power, freeing humans to do what we do best, i.e., sense-making.
- Blockchain: We can now generate much greater security of data transmission, which promotes communication and collaboration, but also secrecy.
- Crowdsourcing: New concepts and platforms enable us to harness ordinary people in efforts to secure society.

These technologies have made information much more visible and available than it was in the past. Information is also "social," in the sense that it is produced and shared by many people; it is local, in that it is geographically tagged; and it is portable, in that it is produced and collected by a wide range of online sensors—most of which are commonly available and easy to use.[23]

Humanity has quickly adapted to these technologies and made them ubiquitous. It took the airline industry sixty-eight years to gain 50 million users. It took electricity forty-six years to reach that number. But it took Facebook only three years, and Twitter only two.[24] How long will it take for people to widely adopt the IoT?

Indeed, these users now include devices, not just people. By 2025, the network giant Cisco estimates that the Internet of Things will have 100 billion nodes.[25] Already in 2016, James Clapper, the former U.S. DNI, said "Agencies will probably use the IoT for identification, surveillance, monitoring, location tracking, and targeting for recruitment, or to gain access to networks or user credentials."[26]

Where will we store that endless amount of data? To answer that question, we will need to understand just how much data we are talking about. Today's data scientists use yottabytes (250 trillion DVDs) to describe how much government data the intelligence agencies have on people altogether. In the near future, brontobyte will be the measurement to describe the type of sensor data that the IoT will generate. Clearly, the burden of data storage will be great, but it may not be so expensive. Data storage costs have been declining dramatically over the past forty years. The space per unit cost has been roughly doubled every fourteen months This gradual doubling has led to incredible results: the cost of storing one gigabyte, back in 1980, was $437,000; today the same gigabyte can be stored for $0.019—a drop in price of 20 million times. If this rate of improvement carries on into the next decade, it will seem much more conceivable to store all those yottabytes of information.[27]

AI will enable us to analyze this flood, as it will scale up as our data trove grows. Artificial neural networks function better when they are trained on larger data sets. AI, in turn, will allow us to collect and analyze even more data. As for computing power, here is an amazing fact: compared to 1955, transistors are now 10,000 times faster and 10 million times cheaper—that's a hundred-billion-fold improvement over the past sixty years.

It isn't surprising, therefore, that the global powers have set achieving technological dominance, if not supremacy, at the heart of their national security strategy. Even a small country such as Israel has formed a national AI center. The race for technological supremacy, most notably AI, is our age's space race, only this time, on steroids It was Vladimir Putin, Russia's strongman, who said, "Whoever becomes the leader in this sphere will become the ruler of the world."[28]

The race for information supremacy is not new, but in the 1990s and early 2000s it focused on battlefield operations. (See the U.S. Army Information Operations Field Manual from 1996, a manifestation of the then new concept of the information age.[29]) Now information superiority will enable countries to gain power over each other. It could even enable nonstate actors to gain unusual power in specific situations, breaking up the monopoly of large states. Current and emerging information technology is accelerating the development of communication means and the technologies of collecting, processing, and storing information. It is also intensifying the "globalization infrastructure" and thereby influencing international dynamics.

Technological progress generates new conditions in which states exercise their sovereign rights and pursue their interests, both in domestic and foreign policy. Already in today's conflicts, digital technology rivals conventional military weapons and tactics. Battlefields will be much bigger, encompassing civil and even psychological arenas, and weapons will be much more diverse, not just limited to kinetic power. States will exercise their sovereign rights and pursue their interests, in domestic and foreign policy, in new ways.

This wider battlefield is why Lieutenant General Robert Ashley, director of the Defense Intelligence Agency (DIA), said (2018) that the United States can no longer rely on its military supremacy. He urged the United States to focus on building new abilities, rather than boost existing ones, as countries that excelled in implementing emerging technologies would enjoy overall superiority. Information technology itself would not guarantee victory, he said, but only those who mastered it would be able to overcome the fog of war in the battlefield.[30]

In such a context, intelligence—developing actionable knowledge for decision making—plays as important a role as ever. But intelligence establishments around the world are now stuck in an existential dilemma, or what some call an epistemological crisis.[31] They are losing an essential attribute: absolute supremacy in the technologies of discovering secrets and the prestige associated with that. Small states and rogue groups, or even benign groups, can hack into financial records and draw on Google Earth to get information that only the CIA and KGB could obtain only a decade or two ago. Policy makers looking for hidden information can get such material from outside sources.

In 2011, the United States finally declassified the Hexagon KH-9 Reconnaissance Satellite, which operated from 1971 to 1986 and had capabilities unmatched across the world. Today, many countries—China, India, South Korea, Japan, France, Germany, and Israel—enjoy these advanced capabilities. The private sector employs an abundance of satellites, including from companies such as the American DigitalGlobe or the French SPOT, which provide high-resolution color satellite imagery. Canada, Germany, and

Italy have launched advanced commercial satellites that include radars and can take pictures at night or through clouds. These commercial satellites are now capable of mapping huge areas for a variety of needs.

In April 2020, the National Geospatial-Intelligence Agency (NGA) published a report that analyzes the use of commercial satellites and associated technologies, and the consequential rise in imagery data. The NGA argued that "today, with commercial GEOINT available worldwide, we face a much more level playing field." The then-NGA chief technology officer, Mark Munsell, wrote in an introductory note, "Several near-peer adversaries are investing significantly in new technologies to close the gap with U.S. and allied capabilities." To stay ahead of these adversaries, the report argues, the NGA must bring together world-class experts at the agency, industry partners with exquisite domain expertise and technical capabilities, and companies that have never worked with the government before but whose products could help advance NGA's mission. To maintain leadership in this realm, the NGA plans to foster partnerships with other agencies, industry, and academia.[32]

In signal intelligence (SIGINT), private companies have likewise developed military-level surveillance technology. NSO, for example, sells hacking tools for mobile devices and online services to government intelligence and security agencies and possibly also to nongovernmental entities.[33] Technologies that recently were the domain of advanced countries are today an off-the-shelf product available to all.

Besides losing their technological supremacy, agencies are struggling to merge the flood of available information into a single intelligence product. Intelligence organizations are giving new attention to cooperation and decentralization. The private sector offers a variety of tools, from simple off-the-shelf solutions to sophisticated tools that enable complex organizational processes. Some of the tools can be purchased and quickly implemented, such as knowledge-sharing platforms, whereas others must be adapted by the organizations themselves to meet their specific needs. As a result, the boundaries between intelligence organizations and the civilian sector are already blurring.

To break out of this crisis, agencies must go beyond Lahneman's vision. Besides working closely with universities, corporations, and startups, they'll need to reach out to counterparts in friendly nations. Instead of a closed intelligence cycle, with analysts fed by collection units, they must engage closely with the outside world, just as any academic or industry analyst would when consuming information.

More important, to manage the information flood, they must end their long-standing emphasis on "neutral," apolitical information and facts, and work with policy makers to develop practical understandings of threats. In a related point, agencies have long prized their ability to describe an ultimate reality based on "objective" facts, if only they would find the right source. Indeed, agencies like to stick to revealing secrets because they think it gives them uniqueness. Policy makers love the access to classified information, and agencies can use this uniqueness to call for more funding. ("I can answer that question, or give you earlier information, only if you raise my budget for sensors," etc.) But the mystique around intelligence agencies is now eroding, and decision makers can now be fed by other credible (and much cheaper) sources.

The flood of information also makes it difficult, if not impossible, for agencies to prioritize which types of information to collect, process, and deliver to analysts. A related problem is that data collection becomes part of the analytic task, not a distinct, neutral act. Both functions must ask questions that will lead to new knowledge and new conceptual categories.

Agencies will also have to deal with the unfortunate blurring of boundaries between real and fake knowledge. Adversaries can use digital technology to develop convincing fakes to disrupt intelligence efforts. That same technology, as seen in the Russians' efforts to influence Western elections, can also weaken fundamental national institutions. If we are entering a "post-truth" era of declining national trust, then intelligence agencies will need to engage with a broad array of stakeholders, not just policy makers. Citizens still want national security, but they're less willing to devote taxes to pay for it, and they worry about privacy. Intelligence organizations will have to find ways to ease their fears and harness their collective wisdom.

Finally, the rapid pace of change undermines two operational tenets of agencies: asking the right question to ignite the intelligence cycle's "engine" and keeping the entire cycle whole and complete. Collecting information, processing and analyzing it, and delivering a full picture is a long process that rarely adheres to the actual pace of the changing reality. Above all, to get there, agencies will have to overcome their industrial logic, centered on the annual intelligence cycle.

Let's go into detail on just why the industrial model no longer works for intelligence agencies. But before we do, we need to explain why the concept is so powerful and why intelligence organizations worldwide find it so hard to abandon the concept. The intelligence cycle presents in a clear way the rationale for missions, structures, and processes, including how the agency interacts with its environment and various stakeholders.

So far, despite many attempts, no one has come up with a replacement model. Even when the U.S. military intelligence developed a more collaborative and agile approach in fighting terrorists in Iraq and Afghanistan (as we will describe later), the overall intelligence paradigm didn't change; it merely tolerated this "local initiative" while containing it so it didn't challenge the organizational mainstream.

One reason for the difficulty of replacing the industrial model is that digitization is undermining geographic borders and traditional organizational barriers. Take, for example, an attempt to hack a system, collect information, and plant a malicious code: it would be hard to differentiate between collecting the data needed for such an operation, the actual act of penetrating the system, and the act of planting the code; or collecting information by participating in closed online social groups in social media platforms, forums, the dark Web, and elsewhere. The act of getting into the group using an alias, operating under disguise while being constantly watched and observed by the group's members, collecting relevant information and analyzing it, or even disseminating false or manipulated data—all require a certain skill set that cannot be set under the intelligence cycle's traditional definitions and functions.

Finally, agencies need a variety of new skills altogether. To handle the flood of data, agencies must move to sense-making, which is less objective and more relational than the traditional approach to knowledge development, so it requires collaboration with the consumers of intelligence knowledge. Agencies must learn how to speak more forcefully and creatively about a situation, rather than limit themselves to the facts—without compromising their credibility and becoming politicized. They need new kinds of talent and communication, which the intelligence cycle usually tends to neglect.[34]

To capture more systematically the key challenges ICs face in this day and age, let's highlight the following arguments:

- New technologies coming to fruition pose a set of major challenges for ICs.
- A first set of challenges relate to the exponential growth of data, which requires agencies to collect, store, and analyze data in unprecedented amounts.
- To that flux of data, we should add false or misinformation and related activities that adversaries carry out. That, in turn, makes the tasks of data processing and sense-making even more challenging.
- Another aspect of the proliferation of old and new types of data is that ICs are losing their monopoly over sense-making for decision-making purposes. The result is growing competition over decision-makers' attention.
- Related to that, the availability of data allows decision makers to be much more knowledgeable about the details of the phenomena they are concerned with. Decision makers now expect their IC to transcend the information-reporting level and provide them with new types of deliverables.
- Finally, the main internal challenge for the IC is to generate a new conceptual framework, one that will replace the outdated concept of the intelligence cycle. As we shall see, a single unified framework is almost

impossible to create, given the dynamic—if not chaotic—nature of the current and future environment in which the IC operates.

This chapter lays out the need for transformation. Fortunately, some important changes are already happening, at least conceptually, and we will explore them later. It is high time that intelligence organizations went through the same revolution the private sector has gone through; that is, harnessing advanced digital tools for accelerating research and development, broadening inter- and intra-organizational collaboration, and turning large hierarchical organizations into agile and dynamic ones. Having won the Cold War, and so far, kept terrorists from disrupting daily life, Western intelligence agencies can congratulate themselves on developing a powerful model of operations. But their success should not lead them to think that digital technologies can be managed as they have handled earlier breakthroughs. These powerful capabilities are fundamentally changing the game for agencies, and they won't maintain their effectiveness unless they act very differently from how they act now. Just how differently is what the rest of the book will explain. But first we must describe the ramifications of digital technologies in more detail.

Chapter 4

Emerging Technologies and the National Intelligence Enterprise

To understand the urgency for transforming intelligence agencies, we need to delve into the exponential technologies mentioned in the previous chapter. These interrelated advances were science fiction only until recently, and they are now solid enough to change how we carry out national intelligence.

This chapter focuses on the Internet of Things (IoT) and 5G technologies that use advanced storage through the cloud, big data analytics to make sense of the resulting flood of information, AI to retrieve insights from that flood, crowdsourcing for further expanded data collection and analysis, and block-chain for secure communication. It also explores quantum computing, which will dramatically boost data processing, encryption, and decryption but is not likely to become practical until the 2030s. I will discuss each technology in turn, but the divisions among them are a bit arbitrary, and policy makers need to consider them holistically. I have skimped on the technical details of the technologies to focus on the implications for intelligence.

This list leaves out other breakthroughs such as biotechnology, which will create new threats to national security but probably will not fundamentally change how intelligence agencies work.[1] I would rather focus on technologies that force agencies to revisit and potentially redefine their own DNA.

My arguments can be summed up fairly simply. Traditionallly, intelligence agencies put much of their efforts into collecting hard-to-get data. The technologies discussed in this chapter will make it far easier to collect, store, process, and analyze data, as well as conduct intelligence operations along with a variety of other national security-related activities. The more that agencies rely on these technologies, managed by trained employees, the more time, budget, and attention they will free up for what humans excel in: interpretation, sense-making, and decision-making. These technologies will thus redefine the profession of intelligence, as well as the structure of intelligence agencies. However, we need to keep in mind that the real promise of such technologies lies within our ability to synthesize technological capabilities, for example, by using AI and blockchain to allow crowds to better collaborate. It is imperative, therefore, that these technologies are examined holistically.

THE INTERNET OF THINGS AND CLOUD STORAGE

IoT has been around for several years but is now practical enough for broad usage. It involves putting networked sensors in or on ordinary physical objects. The sensors can capture simple digital information, such as metrics on an operation, or record audio and take photographs. So, they can capture information on both their own processes and on events around them. Then they transmit this data to other devices or to the cloud. From pavement tiles to concrete blocks in walls, from shoes to clothes, and even our toothbrushes, all can be connected to the internet. In the very near future, information will be streamed from every street, every car, every house, and even from the sky.

IoT will, therefore, generate enormous amounts of data. With 75 to 100 billion connected devices by 2025, research company IDC estimates that data generated from these devices could reach almost eighty zettabytes by that year.[2] One zettabyte equals 1 billion terabytes. You can alternatively think of it as the equivalent of 250 billion DVDs, or 36 million years of HD video.

Endless information is only part of the equation. Where will we store it? Fortunately, data storage costs have declined dramatically over the past forty years. It cost more than US$400,000 to store one gigabyte in 1980; in 2020, it cost two cents.[3] This improvement is likely to continue, with help from cloud computing to allow us affordably to store all those zettabytes. Intelligence agencies will upload large quantities of data to the cloud, store it, and retrieve it as needed. The fifth generation of mobile network technologies, known as 5G, is making transfers of even large volumes of data nearly instantaneous with greater speed, security, and capacity.[4] A few serious issues are preventing large-scale adoption and still being worked out.[5]

Cloud storage potentially offers more data security, not less. For example, it avoids a familiar danger for intelligence agencies: laptop and hard-drive theft. Without cloud storage, a user who loses her computer would also hand over all the data on that device. With it, a lost computer jeopardizes little or no information. Cloud storage could also facilitate data sharing across agencies, and—when combined with other technologies—could potentially prevent the kind of intelligence gaps that happened before the 9/11 terrorist attacks. That is why the U.S. government gave Amazon Web Services a $600 million contract in 2013 as part of a ten-year deal—a project dubbed JEDI—Joint Enterprise Defense Infrastructure;[6] and the CIA has awarded in late 2020 part of its potentially multibillion-dollar Commercial Cloud Enterprise (C2E) contract to five of the largest cloud services providers: Amazon, Google, IBM, Microsoft, and Oracle.[7]

With cloud storage, agencies can also outsource entire networks and data centers, saving physical space, infrastructure, and labor costs.[8] Overall, cloud storage—and generally cloud computing—offers much promise for intel analysts working in national security. Concerns regarding security and privacy are appropriate, but as legal scrutiny and technological understanding increase among government officials, the service will be more and more accepted as time goes on.

The American IC currently is seeking to go beyond the capabilities of cloud servers. To this end, DARPA launched a project called molecular information storage (MIST), which aims to develop technologies for storing data on DNA molecules or other polymeric structures. The advantage of a DNA molecule is that the relatively dense structure of the molecules makes it possible to store an enormous amount of data in minimal space. Not only is the storage of data on these molecules more efficient, but the data will also last longer; up to hundreds of years.[9]

BIG DATA ANALYTICS

In 2013, Edward Snowden, a former employee of the U.S. National Security Agency (NSA), leaked information about the organization's classified surveillance programs. NSA was collecting data not just from potential terrorists but from nearly all U.S. citizens, including everyone surfing the Web. Almost every cell phone call, e-mail, and text was recorded and analyzed by the agency. These records amount to vast, almost unimaginable, quantities of data, kept at huge underground data storage centers in Utah deserts, with minimal processing.

Of course, people, as talented as they may be, are no longer able to process these quantities of data without assistance; they need a machine that is "smart" enough to draw conclusions and identify patterns. In the section dealing with AI, we will review major developments in the area of these "smart" machines.

The main challenge for agencies related to big data is to extract practical and relevant insights and conclusions from the mass of available data. One characteristic of big data is that, for the most part, individual facts and figures are meaningless; insights are generated from the aggregate value of the data. In other words, big data provides another means by which to obtain meaningful information that solves an analytical problem, which is not dependent on the ability to achieve "full" and "objective" knowledge. The other side of the coin is the relative nature of the data: only data from which knowledge can be derived is relevant; and relevance is determined at any given moment, as required. As discussed above, the fact that data can be collected and stored almost without limitation, without immediate processing, and can be recalled if and when a particular need arises, is a unique characteristic of the era of big data.

Another challenge is the need to aggregate different types of data—for example, geographic information, textual information, graphic information—and to derive insights from the aggregate value. This, of course, is not an issue only for intelligence organizations—it is a characteristic of large companies and organizations that collect a range of data from various sources. But the challenge intensifies in an environment that embodies the principle of compartmentalization and sharing on a need-to-know basis. This, and the challenges previously outlined, are expected to intensify in the face of the growing proliferation of sensors in everyday life, as manifested mainly in IoT; and due to the limitations of existing technology, including media channels, in differentiating between fact (real information) and fiction (misinformation). Big data analytics is therefore improving quickly, driven by burgeoning demand from the private sector.

Any company that collects data in large volumes—as does almost every company in this era—encounters these challenges. Thus, it is not surprising that the data analytics market, which involves identifying, interpreting, and communicating data patterns, is growing at an astonishingly fast rate: Global Industry Analysts, a research firm, estimates that it is currently worth about US$130 billion; by 2027 it is expected to grow at a CAGR (compound annual growth rate) of 10 percent to more than $230 billion.[10]

Intelligence agencies can draw on those advances to address four categories of questions: Descriptive—what happens; diagnostic—why what happens happens; predictive—what may be and how likely; and prescriptive—what can be done. Agencies are used to answering such questions from methods in the natural and social sciences: first come up with a hypothesis about the world, then test the hypothesis with empirical data. But thanks to the advances described in this chapter, big data analytics turns this method on its head, because this standard scientific method holds that one must first raise a hypothesis or formulate a theory, then examine the validity of the theory in real terms.

However, in a revolutionary experiment published in 2009, Google researchers asked a computer to discover early indicators of a flu outbreak. The computer skipped the hypothesis stage and simply crunched a mass of data on Google search requests. The computer identified the search terms that best correlated with flu, and the researchers used those terms to predict the following year's outbreaks before anyone else.[11]

The research backed up a remarkable 2008 opinion column by Chris Anderson, editor of *Wired* magazine. In his column, "The End of Theory: The Data Deluge Makes the Scientific Method Obsolete," Anderson suggested that organizations (and I will add, including intelligence agencies) no longer needed to formulate hypotheses, models, or theories:

> There is now a better way. Petabytes allow us to say: "Correlation is enough." We can stop looking for models. We can analyze the data without hypotheses about what it might show. We can throw the numbers into the biggest computing clusters the world has ever seen and let statistical algorithms find patterns where science cannot.[12]

The flood of data fundamentally changes the process of gathering intelligence. The scientific method of testing hypotheses matches the behavior of human cognition—but not how computers work. It is much easier for a computer to analyze all of the data, however much, and to identify hidden patterns, rather than start speculating for an answer.

This approach runs counter to the so-called old guard of intelligence services that Cold War conceptions inspired. They believe that a computer, however powerful, can never replace the human mind, especially our capacity to make judgments and have insights. The truth is that even the most ardent advocates for technology-assisted intelligence do not advocate for removing human involvement. Rather, they call for altering the dynamic between humans and machines and removing humans from certain activities in which their power is negligible when compared with that of computers—and put them to work more on using their judgment and interpretation skills, and developing insights.

Throughout time this data-crunching approach will only get better. Researchers in both the public and private sectors are improving big data analytics by better organizing the data flood and detecting correlations. The U.S. Defense Advanced Research Projects Agency (DARPA) is sponsoring work to map patterns of human behavior, including algorithms that can assist systems, individuals, or groups to quickly identify risky anomalies. DARPA's systems attempt to identify relationships between entities (including people and machines) and can identify, catalog, measure, and monitor the spread of ideas on social media. They can also automatically analyze images and movies.[13]

Other analytic systems assess language to discover sentiments for correlation with other phenomena: Already in 2017, RAND published a study describing a computer program developed for the purpose of analyzing behavioral patterns using big data. According to the publication, the software was developed as a joint venture by a behavioral science expert and an expert in computer science; the former used insights on language to explain unique phenomena and texts, and the latter used an opposite process, first identifying the unique characteristics of the text and then looking at the broader picture to formulate insights.[14]

In the private sector, the most significant company in the field of analytics, particularly in the realm of security, is Palantir (whose investors include the CIA's In-Q-Tel fund), which at some point was valued at about US$40 billion.[15] The company offers software to scan various data sources, including financial documents, airline tickets, cell phone records, and social media publications, looking for links that human analysts cannot identify, and presents the information visually and dynamically.[16]

ARTIFICIAL INTELLIGENCE

In the broadest sense, AI refers to the ability of machines to perform all actions that humans (and animals) can perform. Narrower definitions refer to a machine's ability to perform specific tasks;[17] to machines capable of perceiving their surroundings and, based on this perception, to act in a way that maximizes the chances of achieving the objectives of the operation; or to how machines mimic people's cognitive abilities, such as studying or solving problems.[18]

In practice, machines achieve one of three levels of AI:

1. The first is the development of system expertise, through translation of human knowledge into simple conditions (e.g., if the source is unreliable, then the data is unreliable). The main disadvantage of this approach is that it is resource intensive, because it requires the definition of a large (if not infinite) number of conditions/rules, as well as the need to update them in real time.
2. The second approach involves attempts to allow the machine to plan and perform various actions, such as identifying, from several available options, the optimal path to travel between two points. Although the design of these systems still requires the definition of conditions (as in the first approach), such systems already imitate human intelligence, to some extent, and draw conclusions that are not necessarily intuitive.[19]
3. The third approach involves machine learning, based on repeated queries of dynamic databases, in a way that generates new knowledge.

Data is the lifeblood of AI, as it forms the basis of machine training. In an age of data overload, its availability is not a problem, and it is unlikely to be a problem in the foreseeable future—especially in view of the increasing connectivity and growing availability of mobile devices and sensors of various types. Another engine of AI, the algorithm, is a systematic and unambiguous method of performing a task in a finite number of steps. This engine is also expected to continue to advance, particularly due to large investments made by governments and the private sector, as well as the continued implementation of crowdsourcing and open-source practices that encourage innovation among large and diverse programming communities. These two sub-trends relate to human ability to perfect the algorithms behind the machines. But recently, we have been informed of new machines capable of programming on their own—and in the near future, even developing algorithms.[20] This is another example of learning by the most advanced kind of machine.

Another interesting development is algorithms that can "argue" with one another, or that present different "opinions." As I shall discuss later, this will be the next evolution of crowdsourcing—machines that collaborate with other machines as well as with humans. Google's AutoML is probably one of the most advanced developments in that direction and a crucial step in the development of human thinking, hence a necessary step in achieving a nonstatistical AI.

Probably the most impressive development in the field of AI in recent years is Generative Pre-trained Transformer 3 (GPT-3)—a language model that uses deep learning to produce humanlike text. GPT-3, introduced in May 2020, is the third-generation language prediction model in the GPT series (and the successor to GPT-2) created by OpenAI, a San Francisco-based AI research laboratory.

GPT-3 has a capacity of 175 billion machine learning parameters, which grants it a higher level of accuracy relative to previous versions with smaller capacity. Although still in its infancy, the possibilities of using GPT-3 in various contexts are unimaginable: People have used it to correspond with historical figures via e-mail, write an article about AI being harmless to human beings, generate text-based adventure games, mimic Neil Gaiman's style, and create a short story, as well as generally converse with AI-powered machines.[21]

GPT-4, which likely will be released in the next year or two, will be even more impressive: it may be capable of true reasoning and understanding and a major step toward achieving artificial general intelligence (AGI). The Chinese, on their part, are not lagging behind: in mid-2021 a team at the Chinese company Huawei detailed what might be the Chinese-language equivalent of GPT-3: PanGu-Alpha—a 750-gigabyte model that contains as many as 200 billion parameters—25 million more than GPT-3.[22] A bit later that year, the Beijing Academy of Artificial Intelligence (BAAI) released its "Wu Dao"—a multimodal AI system that can generate text, audio, and images that was trained using 1.75 trillion parameters, compared to GPT's 175 billion.[23]

The quality of the text that GPT-3 and similar models generate is so high that it is difficult to distinguish from that written by a human, which has both benefits and risks. Just imagine the implications for intelligence agencies: on the negative side, adversaries can take deepfake to the next level and produce almost authentic artifacts, such as documents, thus deceiving analysts. On the positive side, GPT-3 and future generations of such language models could make analysts almost obsolete, as they could be used to generate intelligence reports with little to no human involvement.

AI will take big data to the next level of sophistication. Machines will learn over time and make ever better correlations. They will draw conclusions from data and apply them to new situations, all without predetermined rules. By learning from large amounts of data, machines can essentially teach themselves with only partial intervention from humans.

AI also enables a machine to make sense of natural human language, written and spoken, and to communicate with that language. The machine learns how to process this informal information in a structured way, then reproduce it in an unstructured way that people can understand. Going further, with deep learning, machines will better mimic human neural networks (as in the human brain) to make forecasts, which in the context of national intelligence could empower human analysts.

AI may also involve the use of robots. In popular culture, robots take the form of humanlike machines, but in practice they now take various forms and have a variety of uses, including bomb disposal, automated answering services, cleaning, and surgery. This has tremendous implications for national security. In the next few years, AI and robots will not only integrate into human systems on the battlefield, but also accelerate the transition from human-based warfare to unmanned warfare. For example, the Russian Military Industrial Committee has approved a plan that states that by 2030, 30 percent of Russian military combat troops will be based on robotic systems.[24]

The transition to autonomous battlefield systems is in its infancy, but the market for robotic commercial and military applications is growing exponentially while the price per unit is falling. Take drones, for example, which went from being used by only a handful of militaries to becoming a shelf product sold in toy stores at an affordable price. Extensive use of machine learning, combined with market growth and falling prices, will dramatically affect the distribution of AI-powered robots. For example, miniature drones that can be printed by 3-D printers may allow armies to flood the battlefield with thousands (if not hundreds of thousands) of tiny insect-sized drones, as expressed in the concept of offensive swarm-enabled tactics (OFFSET).[25]

The availability of drones, as a case study of the growing proliferation of smart, AI-driven robots, benefits not only conventional armies, but also—and perhaps mainly—nongovernment actors such as guerrilla and terrorist organizations, as well as criminal organizations. However, we can assume that although the absolute power of the parties involved in conflict (armies and nongovernment actors) is likely to rise, the balance of the relative power of nation-state militaries will not change dramatically.[26]

For now, the size, weight, and power of existing computers limit the progress of autonomous systems, but this reality is likely to change, just as smartphones now perform tasks that once only supercomputers were able to perform. As such, in the medium-term future, autonomous robotic systems will be capable of performing complex tasks in combination with abilities found in nature—such as, for example, bringing together a bird's brains, eyes, ears, and wings—a combination that today's autonomous systems cannot reach, certainly not in a coordinated and synchronized manner, on one platform. Robotic insects may in the future integrate such sensors and link intelligence capabilities (mainly in the field of information collection) with operational capabilities.

In the context of data supremacy, intelligence organizations around the world already gather more data than they can process. Indeed, this has been the case since the early 1960s. In fact, it is true for every human from birth. Our senses absorb much more information than our brains can process. But in this day and age, this trend has intensified to a whole new level. Using AI machines will likely solve this problem. For example, AI provides a means to interpret aerial photographs and satellite imagery with minimal human supervision. Image processing systems are already widely used in intelligence organizations, as well as in private companies (e.g., Google and its street view system). In fact, image processing is one of the most advanced applications of AI and machine learning, due to the endless amounts of visual data available to train the machine.

But there is great potential, and automated processing systems are also being developed for other disciplines, such as SIGINT (signals intelligence), which uses voice and text processing. Other systems for analysis of unstructured data are also already in use and promise to fundamentally change the way intelligence is processed and examined. AI will fundamentally alter not just the way data is collected and processed, but also the way intelligence analysis is produced. Such analysis includes not just automated text reports, as in San Francisco's Premier AI, but also multidimensional intelligence products that include edited videos embedded in text, or 3-D representations of intelligence purposes—from structures to humans. In the future, algorithms may be permitted to access and use data that intelligence researchers are not permitted to access—which will likely pose additional dilemmas about the adoption of AI-based solutions.[27]

Another development in the field of scientific research may also be relevant to intelligence research. Applications of AI can accelerate the pace of inventions, specifically by automating scientific experiments, for example. Scientists have already developed a robotic system that is able autonomously to generate genome-related hypotheses, conduct scientific biological experiments to test hypotheses, and reach conclusions about those hypotheses. Another example is the ability to synthesize hundreds of thousands of research papers: A partnership between Barrow Neurological Institute and IBM created a system that uses language processing to scan and analyze a large quantity of academic papers on neurodegenerative disease and draw conclusions from their aggregate analysis; the system successfully identified five genes related to the disease.[28] Furthermore, these systems will be able to create and optimize engineering designs using technology such as advanced simulations. Such systems have already been used in the automotive industry for some time now.

The danger of these technologies is that, especially as they become more affordable and widespread, a counter-capability will likely develop to produce counterfeit data that is highly reliable. This, in turn, will lead to the need to refine AI systems to identify such counterfeit data—and so on. This will also affect the role of intelligence organizations, psychological warfare, and data manipulation, as these capabilities, when they are in the hands of government actors, will fundamentally change existing perceptions of the battle for the public consciousness. For example, supercomputers connected to millions of sensors will give unimaginable power to government actors; they will greatly improve their ability to track hostile elements—both locally and abroad. In addition, propaganda will become inseparable from truth, as democratic processes and free press will have difficulty standing up against "fake news."[29]

In this context, it is apparent that the ICs and private sector (companies such as Facebook and Google) are engaged in finding technological solutions to the fake news challenge. Various actors have also called for cooperation and mutual learning between the public and private sectors to cope with this challenge.[30] DARPA has launched a program aimed at developing a technology that would detect fake images used to influence public opinion.[31] IARPA launched a similar competition called the credibility assessment standardized evaluation (CASE), which focuses on intra-organizational aspects of reliability of information. The U.S. Department of Defense has announced that it had completed development of the first forensic tool using AI to find *deep fakes*—fake videos, which are, in fact, produced using machine learning.[32] And in the United Kingdom, in 2018, the British Ministry of Interior unveiled an algorithm that used audio and image analysis to identify videos from the Islamic State's propaganda apparatus. The tool learned from a thousand existing videos, and it succeeded in identifying 94 percent of a new propaganda campaign, with 99 percent accuracy. Critics say the Islamic State can fool the algorithm by adjusting its activities; the developers say they are regularly updating the tool to keep it reliable.[33]

Another application of AI is in the operation of human resources (HUMINT). Some examples of relevant operations include the following: identifying and locating assets for recruitment, as well as developing behavioral models, to then understand deviations from those models, allowing identification of double agents. In this context, we should mention an additional emerging field: behavioral biometrics—an AI-based capability to identify behavioral and physical patterns through which one may identify anomalies. This would allow identification of an imposter through physical characteristics (e.g., different walking), a forged signature, voice recognition, and more.[34] Finally, AI combined with virtual reality (VR) and augmented reality (AR) will enable agents to create simulated environments for future operations, where forces could be trained before being sent to the field.[35] These technologies will also improve command, control, and decision-making capabilities in remote operations.

BLOCKCHAIN

Blockchain is a technology application that secures online activity and authenticates transactions between different parties without a central management entity. The administrator role is replaced by encrypted blocks of information generated through peer-to-peer (P2P) network-based sharing. Blockchain thus provides a platform on which independent entities can agree on blocks of information connected by chain. Each block contains an ID and a hashing of the contents of the previous block, and the blocks connect to each other. This creates a decentralized data structure, with blocks whose contents cannot be changed once they have been determined.

Blockchain has become a fast-growing commercial industry. The worldwide blockchain market was valued at US$6 billion in 2021. It is forecast to grow to $56 billion by 2026.[36] This growth is driven by several factors: the falling prices of development; the growing popularity of cryptocurrency markets; the rising number of ICOs (initial coin offerings); and the strong demand for simpler, faster, and more transparent and secure business processes.[37] As this book goes to press, a new phenomenon related to blockchain technology is emerging, known as non-fungible token (NFT)—a unit of data on a digital ledger (i.e., blockchain), where each NFT can represent a unique digital item, and thus they are not interchangeable. NFTs can represent digital files such as art, audio, video, and other forms of creative work. Although the digital files themselves are infinitely reproducible, the NFTs representing them are tracked on their underlying blockchains and provide buyers with proof of ownership.

The blockchain technology has many potential uses, but above all for transmitting and sharing data, verifying the authors of that data, and guaranteeing that the data has not been tampered with. Although blockchain is best known for Bitcoin and Ethereum, payments are likely to be less important than the data-related functions. Other applications include voting, digital identity, health-care information, distributed cloud storage, and smart contracts.[38]

Blockchain is likely to transform how intelligence agencies share multi-source information. Each step in the intelligence process would have its own local instance of the blockchain ledger for ready and speedy accessibility, and all endorsed ledger updates would be independently applied through synchronization across each node in the intelligence supply chain. Fine-grained security controls ensure that both suppliers and consumers see only the information they are authorized to see.

Blockchain's improved security and verifiability would greatly help intelligence analysts who now struggle with fragmented, incomplete, and even contradictory data. As explained by Tim Olson of IBM:

> Blockchain traces the origin and refinement of intelligence assets throughout their lifecycle and across the intelligence supply chain. It provides the authoritative, tamper-proof current-state and provenance of each entity-of-interest—person, place, thing, and their relationships—from creation to removal in a shared, immutable intelligence asset ledger.[39]

Especially in combination with AI, blockchain could address the problems of data compartmentalization, verification, and security. Agencies usually store sensitive information in different formats (text, video, etc.) indefinitely on corporate servers, and increasingly on the cloud. They face a tension between the need to share information with different organizational functions or organizations, and the need to protect sensitive data obtained through significant effort or even life-threatening operations.

Data integrity is a serious issue for agencies, as malicious actors can tamper with data to influence intelligence analysts.[40] But major companies and research bodies are addressing these and other issues. Google, through researchers at Cornell University, assessed how organizations can use blockchain to train AI machines without revealing the raw data. Each organization trains its machines based on its own unique sources of data but shares the parameters by which the machine is trained and the insights the machine generates.[41] Microsoft's CryptoNets uses *homomorphic encryption* to train deep-learning systems to collect encrypted data, process it, and produce precise, encrypted answers.[42] Such applications likely will fundamentally change the way intelligence organizations classify and share sensitive data. With the mutual creation of intelligence value becoming a key component of intelligence organizations, blockchain with AI could enable agencies to benefit from cooperation without fear of data leaks or endangering sources.[43]

Intelligence organizations often try to prevent access to digital data through physical means. A better approach is to create data capable of protecting itself—data with inherent mechanisms that prevent, or at least protect it, from exposure or manipulation. Similar to DNA in biological systems, a database might have active properties to hinder opening or alteration. It could retain, for a limited time, previous versions of the data and details on recent interactions with users, regardless of any commands given to it. This new approach assigns identity characteristics to the data itself, rather than to the systems on which the data is stored.

Overall, blockchain promises to secure the benefits of the data flood from IoT, big data analytics, AI, and crowdsourcing. Even for data collected automatically, intelligence analysts still need to have confidence in the reliability of data as it was transmitted and stored. And for data collected from other parties, especially parties that distrust each other, blockchain allows those parties still to collaborate.[44]

QUANTUM COMPUTING

In August 2019, a Google researcher "accidentally" released a paper claiming to have achieved quantum supremacy over conventional supercomputers.[45] Google confirmed achieving such supremacy, despite claims that Google did not properly run the experiment.[46] This—and other breakthroughs—move us closer to a radical new digital technology—with special implications for intelligence and national security. Many observers warn that quantum computing will destabilize military and business dealings by breaking any security code we use. But the prospects for national security, and especially for intelligence agencies, may actually be positive.

Quantum computing is based on quantum mechanics, an established if technically complex area of physics that we already use in cellphones, medical scanners, lasers, and superconductors. Even conventional computers rely to some extent on the dynamics of atoms and subatomic particles.

Quantum computing takes these techniques a step further to generate what we might call Moore's Law on steroids. Conventional computers rely on tiny electric components—transistors—that fit on a single chip. By squeez-ing more transistors onto a chip, we've made processors that perform ever more calculations at ever faster speed. Moore's Law held that the number of transistors on each chip would double every two years. Each transistor, at any moment in time, is in either the "0" or the "1" position. We call those 0s and 1s "bits."

Quantum computers, by contrast, use a special kind of transistor that can be either 0 or 1 at the same time. This phenomenon is called superposition. This transistor yields not a conventional bit but a "qubit," and it can hold far more information than a bit.

Qubits do have some drawbacks, as their probabilistic nature makes them so sensitive to temperature and humidity that researchers usually operate them in freezers. Even then they're less reliable than bits. So, any practical quantum computers must include error correction techniques—a big reason why it's taking a while to develop them.

If we can get a quantum computer to work, it will likely put today's super-computers to shame. The Google paper came from the quantum AI lab,[47] run jointly by NASA, Google, and other partners. Those same researchers coined the theoretical trend *Neven's Law* after Hartmut Neven, their direc-tor.[48] If Neven is right, then quantum computers would increase their process-ing power exponentially, not arithmetically. Instead of doubling every two years, they would increase by four times. Let's say both a conventional and a quantum computer start with two transistors on a chip. Both chips double their transistors every two years, so by year five, both have thirty-two transis-tors. But because qubits can handle so much more information, the quantum computer chip is processing more than a thousand items at once, whereas the conventional chip chugs away at only thirty-two.

The Quantum Artificial Intelligence Lab has successfully operated a quan-tum computer well enough to demonstrate its supremacy over supercomput-ers. The computer was a 53-qubit processor called Sycamore. The researchers found that Sycamore solved a number-crunching problem in a few minutes that would have taken the fastest supercomputer (Summit) thousands of years to complete.

This was a limited and highly artificial test—producing correct samples from a random quantum circuit. Quantum computing won't transform the world until we get a general-purpose processor—one with at least a million qubits. At that point, a quantum computer would easily run circles around any conventional computer in existence.

What happens when (or if) we get such a computer? It would have the processing power to devise codes that no computer could break while break-ing into everyone else's codes. Telecommunications, cybersecurity, advanced manufacturing, finance, and medicine are a few industries that will be changed with quantum computers.[49] Some even argue that another emerging technology—blockchain, which is considered to be hacker-proof—would become obsolete in light of the immense computing power of quantum computers.

When national security experts warn that China is pouring billions into quantum research, they have this nightmare scenario in mind.[50] China has launched an explicit strategy to surpass the West through innovation-driven development. The central government is investing heavily in a megaproject for quantum technology. Its National Laboratory for Quantum Information Sciences could emerge as a key center of gravity for future research and development.

Beyond this general threat, the United States and United Kingdom have issued reports (2018) exploring the many military advantages that might result from quantum computing. For example, an adversary might gain advanced gravity sensors, called quantum gravimeters, that could detect a remote moving mass underwater such as a submarine. Other quantum sensors could detect even low-observable aircraft. A quantum computer could quickly search through a vast action space for a specific target that drones could then attack.

Already the United States may be playing catch-up in some aspects.[51] In 2017, Chinese scientists used quantum encryption to send data from its Micius satellite to an Earth-based ground station twelve hundred kilometers away. They later held an encrypted seventy-five-minute video conference with scientists in Vienna, Austria, that extended the distance to seventy-five hundred kilometers, according to press reports.

The good news is that a dominant general-purpose quantum computer won't emerge suddenly. Even with these recent advances, such a computer still looks to be about a decade away. Quantum computing is so technically difficult that we'll see a lot of labs gradually perfecting their machines.

Also, we should be able to defeat a quantum code breaker by simply using quantum computers to develop new, more sophisticated codes. Encrypted communications and transactions will start using quantum-derived codes early enough so they're unlikely to be vulnerable. The transition period may be messy, but we won't wake up one morning and find everything hacked. We'll settle into the same technological arms race of encryptors and hackers that we have now. As for quantum military sensors, there's no reason why we wouldn't develop quantum countermeasures at the same time.

In fact, the Quantum Artificial Intelligence Lab news will only encourage ever more competitors in the race. A recent *Nature* analysis found that private investors had funded at least fifty-two quantum-technology companies globally since 2012.[52] Aside from Google, such giant technology firms as IBM and Hewlett Packard, along with Baidu and Huawei, are doing research in the field.[53] With commercial investors jumping into quantum computing, it's even less likely that a secret government lab will suddenly control the world.

By improving our ability to analyze massive amounts of data, quantum computing could boost national security in many ways. Consider the proliferation of IoT: Say the CIA is trying to find out what's happening in a certain area of national security concern. Assuming it can hack into at least some of those devices, it will have a lot of data to analyze—and it may have only a short time to do so. With a quantum computer, those massive calculations would be no trouble at all.

That's the positive side of quantum computing: It enables the analytics side of intelligence to keep up with the tsunami of data we will get from the IoT. AI, which takes huge amounts of processing power, will also benefit from quantum technology. Imagine a computer taking in a massive amount of constantly changing data, automatically identifying aberrations, and sending out alerts. It would also generate a treasure trove of insights that human analysts would never discover.

Indeed, a quantum computer could be an Orwellian dream: an all-powerful processor that enables governments to monitor everything going on and report deviations. As dramatized in movies such as *Minority Report* and television shows such as *Person of Interest*, advanced computers with AI could drastically undermine human freedom in the interests of making people safer.

That's all the more reason why Western intelligence agencies need to begin their reforms now, rather than wait for the digital revolution to play out. These agencies must have the ability to match their adversaries in the digital arms race without sacrificing our democracy along the way.

Intelligence agencies, like any long-established organizations, will be inclined to take up these technologies within their established processes. But the technologies are so powerful that they change the underlying dynamics of intelligence work. With computers doing most of the work of collecting data and finding patterns, agencies will be free to do fully human activities: making sense of those patterns for our complex world. Eventually they will have no choice but to convert their processes and structures, but they will be in a better position against adversaries if they start transforming their operations now.

The following three chapters present several new theoretical concepts for intelligence organizations. The first two concepts express the need for ICs to redefine their relations with entities in their environments, most notably, decision makers and the general public. The third concept revolves around a new way to structure intelligence work in an information-heavy environment, using several of the technologies previously discussed.

Several underlying themes are shared across the following concepts: First, there is the need to remove barriers and encourage a collaborative approach, externally and internally alike; second, there is the need to rely heavily on the technologies described in the previous chapters; and third, there is the need to rethink traditional concepts—most important, the one of the intelligence cycle. As such, these new concepts suggest a radical approach to intelligence transformation. It is important to note that such concepts do not exist in a vacuum; they are already being implemented—although partially—across ICs throughout the world. The purpose of the next three chapters, therefore, is to root these concepts in a holistic approach and tie them to the technologies, challenges, and opportunities previously discussed.

Chapter 5

Intelligence Professionals and Decision Makers

A Collaborative Approach[1]

In most—if not all—countries mentioned in this book, the intelligence–decision-maker relations have experienced ups and downs throughout modern history. Decision makers have different views of the role and functioning of intelligence communities in the context of the national security enterprise; and for better or worse, these views have shaped these complex relations. It seems, however, that former U.S. president Donald Trump brought this complex relationship to its lowest ebb, to the point of depreciating the status of the American intelligence community. Indeed, some of Trump's criticism of the U.S. intelligence services is justified and reflected serious underlying problems from which the IC suffered—and still suffers. Unfortunately, these problems are also apparent in other countries surveyed here.

During his term in office, the former U.S. president repeatedly attempted to appoint cronies to key positions in the national security establishment and oust those who refused to align with him. Trump's animosity toward the intelligence establishment was underscored by a series of actions: in January 2017, amid leaks from the investigation into Russian involvement in the 2016 presidential election, he claimed that conduct by American intelligence was reminiscent of Nazi Germany. In May 2017, he fired FBI director James Comey. In May 2018, Trump claimed that the intelligence organizations had been illegally surveilling him. In August 2018, he revoked former head of the CIA John Brennan's security clearance after the latter criticized him. In January 2019, after the Annual Threat Assessment of the U.S. intelligence community was presented to Congress, Trump tweeted that intelligence personnel were "passive and naive" and suggested that they "go back to school." Then, in May of that year, Attorney General William Barr began probing the intelligence community's investigation into Russian involvement in the 2016 election; in July, Trump fired Director of National Intelligence (DNI) Dan Coats; and on February 28, 2020, Trump announced his intention to appoint John Ratcliffe as the new DNI. Ratcliffe had previously attacked the intelligence community's conclusions about Russian involvement in the 2016 election, making it unsurprising that the former president would take a liking to him.

Trump is, of course, not the first president to appoint loyalists to key positions, including positions in the intelligence community. To a large extent this makes sense: The president must trust whoever they appoint to the most sensitive positions and feel comfortable with partners in realizing the head of state's vision and strategy. But the charged relationship between the former president and his intelligence community indicates a deeper crisis that intelligence communities around the world have experienced and continue to experience—albeit to a lesser extent than the extreme case that occurred in the United States.

The crisis in the United States stemmed from the former president's vocal objection to the three most basic foundations of the intelligence enterprise: first, the emphasis on facts; second, expertise as a key component in the interpretation of reality and in drawing relevant conclusions for decision making; and, third, the need to involve intelligence personnel in the decision-making process at the national level. Trump repeatedly expressed skepticism about the facts that the intelligence community provided and questioned the expertise and skills of his intelligence personnel in collecting and interpreting information. Beyond that, he challenged the place of intelligence in decision-making processes—a problem that rose to the surface in all its severity during the COVID-19 crisis (see chapter 9). Trump lied and distorted data that the intelligence community presented to him, dismissed views contrary to his own, and ultimately directly attacked the most senior echelons of the community. He disagreed with intelligence assessments on North Korea's nuclear program and contradicted the intelligence community's claims that Saudi Crown Prince MBS was involved in the assassination of journalist Jamal Khashoggi.

Trump's allegations have some substance, especially in his criticism of the processes of intelligence creation and communication. He often claimed that the intelligence system is outdated and prone to error; when he took office, he stated that he did not need the daily intelligence briefing because he was "a smart person" who did not "have to be told the same thing in the same words every single day." In other cases, Trump accused intelligence agencies of politicization; of carrying out activities that were not in accordance with regulations—as confirmed by the Department of Justice Office of the Inspector General—and even of illegal actions, including leaks and surveillance intended to damage his image.

Without delving into a debate on the accuracy of his claims, it is worthwhile at this point to review briefly the complex relationship between decision makers and intelligence personnel and draw conclusions for the future. My main argument here is that the abundance of information and the proliferation of platforms and organizations that purport to present facts and interpretations not only undermine the status of traditional knowledge agents (which include intelligence, along with scientific institutions), but also undermine the status of intelligence communities. To maintain relevance in decision-making processes, especially at the strategic level, intelligence services must move away from the perception that their role is limited to interpreting facts and that they must remain detached from decision-making processes to avoid "contaminating" the intelligence product. An approach adapted to the present time sees the intelligence agent as an active partner in the decision-making process, someone deeply connected to the decision maker.

Already in the 1940s, in the early days of intelligence at the national level, debates about the role of intelligence in decision-making processes had emerged. The key debate, then as now, revolved around the question of how closely intelligence personnel should work with political leaders: What is the relationship between an intelligence officer's desire to influence the decision-making process and her primary professional commitment to provide intelligence that reflects the apparent reality? Additional questions have emerged over time, including: Is the central role of an intelligence professional merely to provide intelligence, or to be an active partner in policy design? Is strategic intelligence the product of research bodies in the intelligence community? Or is it, rather, a product of a discourse that both affects and is affected by the political leadership—and that leads to new strategic information that enables the formulation of national policy? What is the best possible way to bridge the inherent gap between decision makers and intelligence practitioners?[2] A related question, which will not be discussed in this book but is worth mentioning nonetheless, is how much intelligence officers should adapt—and even change—their estimates to adhere to the policymaker's agenda or worldview.

Before I present the heated debate about these questions, several definitions are required: First, it is important to characterize strategic intelligence as a product of both research and dialogue between the intelligence professionals and the decision makers. I will use former head of the AMAN research division Itai Baron's definition, according to which national intelligence at the strategic level serves the state's political leadership, which operates at the grand strategy level. This is the level of intelligence required to develop defense doctrine and to design national policy in various arenas. The role of strategic intelligence is to assist leaders in developing worldviews, formulating policy, and making decisions about national defense. Strategic intelligence should, thus, provide assessments that help leaders to understand reality, manage threats, and take advantage of opportunities. It should challenge current policy when intelligence information reveals gaps in the general understanding of the strategic environment following identification of strategic trends and assessment of the role of the observer in the strategic environment of the future.

Generally speaking, there are two main approaches to the desired relation between intelligence officials and decision makers: the traditional approach and the collaborative approach.

THE TRADITIONAL APPROACH
AND ITS CHALLENGES

The traditional approach holds that intelligence should stay as independent of the interests of decision makers as possible; otherwise, it risks becoming one of the many influencing factors in the policy debate. If intelligence agencies influence policy, they are seen as performing a "double sin": First, the intelligence provided is likely to not be "objective" and, as such, is considered to be misleading to policy makers. Second, intelligence loses its authority as the main representation of "reality" in the strategic discussion led by the policy maker.

Early proponents of the traditional approach were William Donovan, Allen Dulles, and Roscoe Hillenkoetter, considered the three founding fathers of U.S. intelligence. They believed that the intelligence community should maintain a certain distance (but not be detached) from decision-making processes—that is, that it should carry out independent research and assessment, and avoid making intelligence judgments tailored to the ideological and political considerations of decision makers.

Yale University professor and intelligence analysis progenitor Sherman Kent also supported this approach at the beginning of his academic career. In 1949, Kent wrote that national intelligence is a "service function" and that the intelligence product would be tainted by the subjective judgments that invariably would result from any direct contact with the consumer. Thus, Kent established the characterization of the intelligence officer as the producer and the leadership as the consumer—two clearly separate functions. Kent emphasized that the intelligence agency is obligated to respond to requests it receives from the policy maker, but it should maintain independence and objectivity in the process.[3]

Kent's description of the producer and consumer was problematic in several respects: First, he maintained that decision makers are naturally skeptical toward intelligence, and that this skepticism is justified by the fact that intelligence officials tend to have limited liability for their intelligence "product"—especially when it comes to predictions. Therefore, Kent argued for the intelligence professional to be an external and objective observer of the phenomenon being studied, with the resulting observations being the basis upon which political leadership makes policy decisions. Too much proximity between the producer and the consumer, Kent argued, infringes on the objectivity of the intelligence, damages the (already-limited) trust the consumer has in the producer, and counteracts the basic purpose of intelligence. To remain relevant, he argued that intelligence agencies should maintain a degree of closeness to the policy maker but avoid being too close to the point of losing objectivity and professional integrity.[4]

Accordingly, Kent proposed a controlled system of contact between intelligence personnel and political leadership. Indeed, in the absence of established communication channels, he believed that discrepancies in expectations would arise between the parties. Kent was concerned that political leadership would set impossible goals for intelligence operations, which would lead to a different approach on the part of intelligence personnel. As such, he advocated establishing mechanisms and institutionalizing workflows to allow the political leadership to effectively guide intelligence operations. Such guidance would build confidence between the two sides and ensure that the intelligence agency could perform its function most effectively.

Earlier in this book, I described Kent's linear *intelligence cycle*, which sees minimal contact between the political echelon and intelligence personnel.[5] Let's recap:

- A strategic problem appears or is identified—discovered through a directive from the political leadership or detection of something extraordinary by intelligence personnel.
- Data about the issue is collected in a targeted manner; this stage, too, is carried out within the intelligence agencies.
- The data is evaluated and critiqued by those involved in the research, comparing the new data with existing knowledge.
- A hypothesis is formulated—that is, an estimation based on the information collected.
- The intelligence product is presented to the political leadership.

Notably, only in the first and final stages do the intelligence personnel and political leadership meet; most of the learning and consideration processes take place within the intelligence system, and the concepts of collaborative learning and discourse are entirely absent.

Throughout the years, attempts have been made to refine the concept of the intelligence cycle, but these efforts have assumed the task of data collection and learning as almost exclusively the role of intelligence; thus, adjustments and updates were made accordingly. For example, Jordan and Taylor added two nonlinear elements to Kent's basic cycle: management and coordination, which form a base around which the six stages revolve.[6]

The post-traditional approach was developed later and differs from the traditional approach in that it does not see intelligence as the only component— nor even necessarily the most important component—in the decision-making process. Jack Zlotnick, for example, made the case for strengthening ties between intelligence personnel and decision makers, given that the former compete with several others for the latter's attention. Thus, he argued, reducing the distance between the parties would give the intelligence personnel greater prominence, giving them a better understanding of the effect of intelligence on the decision-making process—which, in turn, would improve intelligence operations.[7] Moreover, the post-traditional approach incorporates the idea that, aside from describing reality, intelligence should provide policy makers with details regarding the possible future implications of the policy under consideration.

Ultimately, the post-traditional approach continues to stress the need for a clear distinction between the intelligence producer and its consumers, particularly with regard to structural aspects. For example, John Huizinga argued that there is a need for an ongoing dialogue between the two, because intelligence is an inherent part of the decision-making process—but that ultimately, the intelligence agency must present as objective a picture as possible, one that is not influenced by the considerations of the political leadership.[8]

The traditional approaches suffer from several problems that, especially today, make it obsolete. They view knowledge—particularly intelligence knowledge—as "truth" if it accurately represents reality and "right" if it faithfully describes the situation as it is "in reality." This refers to both limited and broad representations, as well as to tangible physical representations and to abstract ones. It involves an extension of the concept of factual knowledge to more abstract realms. A key argument against the traditional approach is the assertion that, contrary to the tactical environment where knowledge is universal (and more objective), in the strategic environment it is not possible to separate an interpretation from the interests of the interpreter.

Another problem relates directly to the concept of the intelligence cycle: in that model, the concept of "collection" (of intelligence information) is a metaphor for a constellation of facts that exist independently somewhere; the intelligence officer's mission is to collect them. From that point of view, the term "processing" expresses the idea that intelligence personnel put the pieces of information together to create a complete picture of the "true" reality. According to this model, intelligence work is equivalent to a puzzle—which allows almost no room for subjective interpretation except analysis or forecasts to fill in any missing pieces.

Thus, the practice of national intelligence as represented by this appproach characterizes the intelligence-leadership relationship as separate and one-sided. In other words, a systematic analysis of the opponent comes before any discussion of policy design. Intelligence personnel are usually required to only present at the beginning of the discussion or provide a written account of their analysis. According to this concept, just like on a battlefield, where intelligence reports come ahead of the operation, the assessment comes ahead of political action in the field of strategic intelligence.

THE COLLABORATIVE APPROACH

In the United States, the close contact between intelligence personnel and policy makers during the 1960s, followed by a series of intelligence failures during the 1970s, led to a departure from an approach that promoted a clear and strict separation between the parties. There were intelligence failures surrounding the Vietnam War, leaks to the press regarding sensitive intelligence operations and revelations that the CIA was carrying out operations (including on U.S. soil) without the permission or knowledge of the political leadership.

These events led to a series of commissions of inquiry that reexamined the work of the U.S. intelligence services and led to development of what we call the "collaborative approach."[9] Committee members recommended the establishment of mechanisms for strengthening relations between intelligence and political leadership beyond the government simply controlling or supervising intelligence operations. This approach suggests opening a channel for direct and personal—even informal—dialogue between intelligence personnel and their "consumers." According to this approach, the relationship between the two parties is symbiotic in nature; therefore, a close working relationship is a must: this relationship is regulated through organizational mechanisms that will ensure the bidirectional transfer of information and feedback.

Willmoore Kendall, then a professor at Yale, published a study in 1949 titled *The Function of Intelligence*, which took issue with the allegations raised in Kent's book published that same year.[10] According to Kendall, the role of intelligence is to assist policy makers to influence and shape reality; thus, he saw nothing wrong with a close relationship between the two but, rather, claimed that such a relationship is necessary and desirable. Like Kent,

Kendall believed that the decision maker must be the party who leads the intelligence operations. But following that assertion, and in contrast to Kent, he claimed that intelligence personnel help policy makers to influence the reality in that they explain how world events affect and may affect national security. As such, Kendall asserted, intelligence personnel cannot separate themselves from their own perspectives, which are integral to their role.

Roger Hilsman, one of the architects of U.S. intelligence doctrine, sided with this approach and argued that intelligence personnel should be encouraged to examine how their analyses affect the range of options available to the decision maker. He claimed that intelligence professionals must not remain detached from those for whom their "product" is intended. Intelligence personnel work for policy makers and serve their purpose only by providing them with the necessary background information for evaluating situations and making decisions[11]—or, as Robert Jervis put it, "intelligence is . . . easier to keep pure when it is irrelevant."[12] According to William Brands, intelligence outputs must be useful to policy makers; as such, the intelligence community must be close to the decision makers to distinctly understand their needs. These needs guide the path of the collection and research efforts—at the same time, a system that allows feedback from the decision makers regarding the intelligence outputs must be maintained.[13]

Similar arguments were presented by policy makers, sometimes as part of the greater need for collaboration between civilian and military echelons.[14] For example, former undersecretary of defense Paul Wolfowitz argued for closer relationships between analysts and policy makers and outlined practices that he believes help the policy-making process.[15]

An example of the adoption of this approach by policy makers is illustrated in a speech given by Robert Gates in 1992, shortly after his appointment as the DCI (director of central intelligence). Gates emphasized the importance of open dialogue in the relationship between intelligence and political leadership, particularly given that none of the parties involved in the strategic debate are infallible: "No one has a monopoly on the truth: We are all learning new things every day . . . dialogue must take place, each participant must be open to new ideas, and well-grounded alternative views must be represented."[16]

Gates asserted that in interactions between the two parties, both sides take equal part in the dialogue and build up the knowledge together, rather than having a one-sided process in which intelligence personnel provide information to the leadership:

> Getting the policymaker to read our products should not jeopardize our objectivity, it does not mean sugarcoating our analysis. On the contrary, it means providing a frank even-handed discussion of the issue. If we know that a policymaker holds a certain viewpoint on an issue that is different from our analysis, we

ought not lightly dismiss that view but rather address its strengths and weaknesses and then provide the evidence and reasoning behind our own judgment.[17]

Several advocated such a collaborative approach within the field of intelligence. G. Murphy Donovan, a former RAND research fellow, discussed how intelligence officers and policy makers coexist in a symbiotic relationship,[18] while Tom Bjorkman, a former Brookings fellow and former IC executive, articulated the benefits of close and continual contact.[19] Robert Cardillo, former director of the NGA, described how the intelligence community's values and goals could only be achieved through better integration with decision makers. He also portrayed a future in which the IC is fully integrated and better positioned to fulfill its missions.[20]

Josh Kerbel and Anthony Olcott present the most updated concept of this approach, asserting the need for a "synthesis" between the parties through which the intelligence agency ceases to be simply a supplier of information and evolves to supply both knowledge and ideas. For decision makers, the change Kerbel and Olcott describe is twofold: they must both trust intelligence officials enough to share policy details with them and get used to asking questions about something more than "data nuggets."[21] Thus intelligence personnel should be involved in formulating recommendations, overcoming a reluctance to do so—a reluctance that prevents them from integrating the implications of military operations into their assessments. In their view, under such conditions of dialogue and cooperation, it would be impossible to refer to "policy successes" or "intelligence failures," as the two would be intertwined.[22]

An additional change foreseen by this method is the need for intelligence personnel to be well-versed in relevant policy and then to adapt intelligence assessments according to the needs arising from that policy. According to Kerbel and Olcott, "Having achieved that status, the synthesis would then at some level accept the policy goal as legitimate and desirable, even though the way in which he or she best serves the client is in arguing—strenuously if need be—about the tactics by which a strategy might be achieved."[23] Indeed, development of such a model—in which intelligence is integrated with policy design—may result in a state of tension between intelligence personnel and policy makers. In cases where an intelligence officer does not identify with the proposed policy, Kerbel and Olcott argue that the officer should resign. In other cases, a lack of tension might allow politicians to use intelligence as a political tool (it is argued that this was the case with intelligence policy in Iraq in 2003).[24]

But in Kerbel and Olcott's view, tension is an essential aspect of the intelligence world and can exist in the same vein that a lawyer can represent a person who undoubtedly has committed a crime (or choose not to represent the person, just as in the intelligence world the officer can resign). The main achievement of this approach, beyond ensuring that intelligence is relevant, is that decision makers will have—if they so choose—partners with whom they can debate, ask questions, and design appropriate policy solutions.

My theoretical framework, through which I approach the intelligence–leadership relationship that should be adopted, emerges from what I (together with David Simantov) have termed "the collaborative approach." This approach is based on the premise that intelligence does not refer only to an objective reality that is independent of the observer—intelligence is not just "an institution for the clarification of reality."[25] The motives of the observer, her values, strategic interests, or even the choice to investigate the issue at hand rather than another—all form part of the basic framework of how reality is interpreted by intelligence personnel.

As such, our foundation emerges in opposition to the concept that sees the collection of data about the strategic environment or opponents to be an exclusive function of intelligence. This approach does not see the intelligence output as a product that emerges at the final stage of the process—that is, a "product" laid on the table of a "consumer"—but as a starting point for the process of developing shared knowledge.

My approach emphasizes three dimensions with respect to the role and operation of national-level intelligence:

1. A departure from the view that the function of intelligence is to clarify the situation through the "discovery" of the truth, as there is no one truth at the strategic level.
2. A departure from the assessment of the quality of intelligence according to its ability to reflect the "objective" reality, instead evaluating its worth on the basis of its relevance to decision making.
3. Emphasis on the need for political leadership and intelligence personnel to develop a partnership and to create the conditions for open dialogue necessary for the development of knowledge, feeding into policy design and implementation.

FROM FACTS TO INTERPRETATION

As outlined, the knowledge required to design a successful strategy is abstract data conceptualized in a tangible context that expresses an idea and interpretation rather than concrete data. Unlike intelligence in the context of the tactical environment, national-level intelligence is developed by intelligence personnel and is not received in the form of an intelligence report.

The challenge for intelligence, according to this collaborative approach, is entirely different from the role assigned to it according to the traditional approach: it is not to obtain and present facts, but to provide an interpretation and conceptualization of the happenings in the enemy's realm as a foundation for productive dialogue with the political leadership—which then serves as a platform for policy development. In most cases, this conceptualization involves a subjective interpretation of the enemy's actions.

Intelligence analysis at the strategic level cannot be deemed "correct" or "incorrect," as it reflects an interpretation that serves the formulation of policy for a specific purpose, rather than universal policy.[26] It is important to emphasize, however, that the transition from facts to interpretations does not entail a complete divorce from the factual component of intelligence work. Interpretation in the strategic environment always relies on facts. In their transition from objectivity to relevancy, intelligence practitioners must maintain their professional integrity. In a collaborative discourse, intelligence officers have the advantage of having direct access to information as well as knowledge of the development processes critical to decision making. Fact and interpretations are two contingent dimensions, both necessary for decision making.

FROM OBJECTIVITY TO RELEVANCE

Although occasionally we hear of approaches that emphasize the importance of relevance rather than objectivity and deny from the outset that objectivity is possible, the prevailing view among the heads of research in the Israeli intelligence community and the United States alike advocates striving for objectivity, despite recognition of the difficulty in achieving such objectivity—or at least in finding the balance between objectivity and relevance. For example, the CIA website highlights the need for an objective analysis: "Members of the [Directorate of Analysis] help provide timely, accurate, and objective all-source intelligence analysis on the full range of national security and foreign policy issues to the President, Cabinet, and senior policymakers in the U.S. government."[27]

As noted, I see the aspiration for objectivity in intelligence at the strategic level as a futile attempt, because knowledge and data will always be relative and depend on the observer. As such, I seek to depart from the principle that examines the quality of intelligence in connection with the idea of objectivity and, instead, replace it with the principle of relevance to the decision-making process. This principle as the benchmark for evaluating intelligence as it applies to policy makers at the national level was presented clearly by Kerbel and Olcott.

FROM THE PRODUCER/CONSUMER DICHOTOMY TO COLLABORATION

Political leadership requires a partner to—together with intelligence—understand the limitations and vulnerabilities of the players in the strategic environment and design a successful policy or strategy in light of those factors. Strategy formulation work, therefore, is a joint operation, led by the policy maker, in which the intelligence officer plays a unique role—presenting an analysis of the strategic environment.

However, the intelligence officer and the analysis that he or she brings to the table are not independent, as in Kent's intelligence cycle but, rather, part of a collaborative process of knowledge development. If the intelligence officer were to provide isolated intelligence insights with no deeper observation or analysis, the process would be significantly deficient. The development of a strategic understanding of an arena or a rival must be a joint effort of intelligence personnel and policy makers.

Thus, I seek to part with the traditional dichotomy that distinguishes between intelligence producers and their consumers, and treat them—at least on the theoretical level—as partners, even if they are not equal partners.

PROBLEMS WITH IMPLEMENTATION OF THE COLLABORATIVE APPROACH

Between intelligence personnel and military leaders, a collaborative approach is common practice—for example, the intelligence officer in command plays an integral part in knowledge development forums led by the general commanding officer.

However, throughout the years, significant difficulties have arisen in efforts to implement the collaborative approach in relations between intelligence and political leadership at the national level. I believe that these difficulties arise from behavioral and structural traits of both political leadership and intelligence officers, as well as from the tensions that are characteristic of the national political arena.

First, there is a basic tension in the strategic environment between the perspectives of some intelligence personnel who are concerned with *describing* the future and the political leadership who are focused on *creating* the future.[28] Policy makers often claim that intelligence personnel tend to increase the level of uncertainty in the political sphere. Intelligence personnel tend to qualify their own analyses, often vaguely describing a variety of scenarios. The political leadership *does* often seek forecasts from intelligence personnel; yet, so long as intelligence agents act only as "prophets," they cannot form complete partnerships with the leadership.

A second significant barrier is that policy makers are reluctant to share their secret considerations and intentions with the intelligence community. They are concerned about leaks, sometimes do not want to be challenged, want to implement a particular worldview, and seek to avoid critique from any professional that might cast doubt on their plans. Dan Meridor, an Israeli former intelligence minister and cabinet secretary during Israeli Prime Minister Menachim Begin's tenure, noted, "Political leaders adopt intelligence reports when they are consistent with their notions and ignore them when they contradict their ideas or may harm their political interests."[29]

An additional problem emerges from a lack of shared language—from the perspective of political leaders, the language used by intelligence personnel is not clear, or at least does not reflect the levels of certainty they seek to manage risks. Other problems stem from the fact that decision makers rely on several sources of information on the strategic environment, the majority of which are from outside the realm of intelligence. This is particularly relevant in the current era, given the large amounts of information that are easily accessible to all, when anyone can provide interpretations and insights and political leadership has its own sources. A political leader might justifiably ask: What added value does the intelligence community bring compared with the several alternative interpretations that are directly available and may be more compatible with our own worldview?

In addition, the policy maker often has an advantage in his comprehension of the strategic system, particularly if the leader in question has significant experience and personal contacts with world leaders, or transferred to politics from a military career. Political leaders usually have a deep understanding of international affairs; this might prevent them from seeing intelligence personnel as partners—particularly if the latter emphasize military threats more than policy opportunities. Finally, although, as noted, intelligence personnel are most likely to focus on military threats, the political agenda is most often focused on civil society. Given that disparity, even if eager to consider the intelligence community as a partner, the political leadership might find it difficult to do so.

To this point, I have described the difficulties and obstacles that often prevent the political leadership from seeing intelligence personnel as partners. Barriers also prevent intelligence personnel from seeing themselves in that light. These include, for example, the fact that the traditional approach is entrenched in the intelligence community. Moreover, the nature of intelligence outputs often does not promote dialogue but, rather, describes end results in a vague manner. The combined presence of barriers in both directions and, particularly, the lack of recognition among intelligence personnel and political leaders that the cooperative approach provides opportunity to open strategic dialogue makes implementation of the approach difficult, if not impossible.

There is no doubt that the political leadership is entitled to accept or reject intelligence assessment, to involve intelligence officers in the decision-making process (or not), and to make decisions according to their worldview. Leaders are political beings, elected in light of specific worldviews, and they have the responsibility of acting in the way that they believe is best for the state. Ultimately, the leadership makes decisions on the basis of a wide range of considerations—for example, commitment to an ideology, political and electoral considerations, and other constraints of which intelligence is just one. As we have shown, leaders often claim that they do not require intelligence assessments, not to mention recommendations from intelligence officers as to the best course of action.

Thus, significant hurdles are in the way of synthesis between intelligence personnel and the political leadership—including the reluctance of decision makers to expose or commit to policy, their concerns regarding leaks, and a tradition of bureaucratic practice. Dogmatic principles of producer–consumer relations—still quite dominant in the discourse on national intelligence—and the endeavor to reach "objectivity" also pose significant obstacles. A structural change in the relations between intelligence officials and policy makers is in its very early stages, but the idea of cooperation between the parties appears to be an appropriate foundation to shape the relations and to ensure an optimal response to the challenges they both face. The preliminary condition for such a change, as Kerbel and Olcott so aptly and simply put it, is first and foremost, a "will to change."[30]

Chapter 6

Opening the Closed Intelligence System

By nature, intelligence organizations are closed organizations. Almost since their inception, they have tended, and continue, to distance themselves from the "outside" world, that is, the private sector and the public (and sometimes even academia and even other governmental organizations) and maintain only essential contact. This is not surprising: the agencies must protect their sources' security, as well as confidentiality of operations and personnel. In democratic regimes they must protect themselves from politicization and preserve a seemingly apolitical approach.

But the trends discussed in this book challenge that long-standing perception: the threats that intelligence organizations face are shifting from classic military and security threats to threats interlinked with the civilian world, including cyber threats aimed at civilian infrastructure, attempts to influence social consciousness, and interference in democratic processes. In the field of technology, as noted, organizations have lost their primacy in leading technological developments to the private sector. The abundance of information also requires the organizations to work with civilian companies that sometimes even own the data. And last, intelligence agencies compete with technology companies over talented, educated, and trained personnel. These companies offer diverse challenges and roles alongside financial reward at levels unattainable in the public sector. Given these circumstances, many of those working within the intelligence community have called for blurring the boundaries between the intelligence community and private companies, public organizations, and the public itself. Moreover, at least in the United States and the United Kingdom, and to a lesser extent in other Western democracies, the intelligence community is showing a greater commitment to openness and to sharing intelligence insights with the public.

In this chapter, I address several aspects of this blurring of boundaries: the deepening ties between intelligence communities and the scientific and technological sectors; the privatization of some intelligence operations, including sensitive ones; the "intelligence" role that the media, groups, and individuals have taken on; and the efforts of intelligence agencies to open direct channels of communication with the public.

THE DEEPENING TIES BETWEEN INTELLIGENCE COMMUNITIES AND THE SCIENTIFIC AND TECHNOLOGICAL SECTOR

In recent years, the American IC, and the British on its heels, have been strengthening their ties with the civilian scientific and technological sectors. The goal is to import "civilian" technologies for intelligence use and to use "civilian" knowledge to protect intelligence assets in cyberspace. I mentioned some of the examples earlier, including IARPA—the intelligence research and development body that bases some of its research and development projects on the private sector, as well as the venture capital created by the CIA, In-Q-Tel, which locates entrepreneurs, start-ups, and technologies that are relevant to the intelligence community from within the private sector. Alongside this, the American community is working with academic institutions to encourage young people to enter STEM professions and is developing new recruitment models, which include significant exchange between the public and private sectors.[1]

But this is just the beginning. In 2019, a research institute belonging to MIT conducted research at the request of the U.S. Department of Defense aimed at helping the latter to improve the synergies between its own research and development bodies and civilian innovation centers in the United States. The institute proposed a series of recommendations centered on prioritizing human resource development, developing a culture that encourages entrepreneurship, promoting collaboration with local entrepreneurs, and building a tolerance for the risk involved in developing new technologies. The institute also recommended contacting venture capital communities, including investors and venture capital funds, to locate funding channels for high-risk, high-reward technological initiatives. Finally, the institute suggested that the Department of Defense provides entrepreneurs with advanced tools and capabilities, for example, by setting up civilian laboratories within campuses that the DoD manages.[2]

It appears that these recommendations are already gaining ground. The National Geospatial Agency (NGA) is currently setting up a second headquarters in North St. Louis, Missouri, known as NGA2West (N2W for short), at a cost of more than US$7 billion. The headquarters, its construction expected to be completed by 2025, is anticipated to house more than three thousand employees. Its location was chosen not only because of its proximity to the existing headquarters, but also because of its central urban setting, near the city's growing start-up scene and academic institutions that will supply future recruits.

The need for an additional headquarters arose from deficiencies and security problems at the existing St. Louis headquarters, built in the 1980s. However, the main consideration behind the new location is related to the agency's desire to make a profound change, in line with technological trends and changes in the labor market. Thus, N2W's vision includes the use of unclassified spaces, an ecosystem that supports the use of mobile and wireless devices, and the creation of collaborative workspaces.[3] Moreover, the NGA is working to expand its collaboration with civil stakeholders in the city, including volunteering and mentoring in local schools; STEM training at public universities; and joint ventures with laboratories, innovation incubators, and accelerators. The industry is keeping up as well, working to leverage the establishment of the new headquarters as a regional growth engine. In January 2020, industry, academia, and the local community launched a joint initiative called GeoFutures that includes a detailed road map for making St. Louis a global hub in the geospatial field—one that will attract technology and information companies.[4] A key technology incubator in the city (T-REX) and Saint Louis University both have established geospatial research centers, and several geospatial-based companies and start-ups have already begun to expand their presence in North St. Louis.[5]

In another case, the FBI has begun to build a US$1 billion campus in Huntsville, Alabama, on an army base, for which it obtained a land permit (special type of lease for federal tenants). Completion of the first phase of the project was completed in 2021, and the complex is expected to absorb fourteen hundred employees, who will join the existing four hundred. Over the next decade, an additional four thousand employees are expected to be added, many of them new recruits. A key attraction for the FBI to Huntsville is that it is a hub for STEM fields—one indicator being that the number of engineers in the city per capita is one of the highest in the United States. Moreover, the industrial-security complex has a massive presence in the area, including military bases and Department of Defense offices, a NASA center, and many companies in the fields of security and space.

Paul Abbate, deputy director of the FBI who heads the project, has stated that on-campus activities will encompass all areas of the agency's operations, and that the agency sees it as a second headquarters and a backup to the existing headquarters. In his words, "It's really the future of the FBI, and it's all about technology, innovation, talent and resiliency."[6] It is clear, then, that in choosing to set up a campus in this area, the FBI seeks to create scientific partnerships with the military, counterpart agencies, academic institutions, and private companies.

The British services are not far behind. In late 2019, the GCHQ inaugurated Heron House in the heart of Manchester, accommodating hundreds of agency staff. According to the agency's website, the new building, centrally located in a thriving technological environment, is designed to bring innovative and groundbreaking technologies to GCHQ and to draw on the talent of the workforce and local companies, particularly in recruiting the next generation of agency staff.[7] The building in Manchester contains a public space that hosts start-ups and local innovation entrepreneurs to collaborate in cracking GCHQ's technological challenges. In addition, the agency has initiated several joint projects in the city, with both academia and technology companies, to solve complex technological challenges, and works with local schools to encourage students to consider a career in STEM fields. According to local industry sources, the very decision of GCHQ to establish a presence in Manchester has already led several high-tech companies, mainly in the cyber field, to move into the area.[8]

These three examples illustrate how intelligence agencies have chosen to set up offices in the heart of scientific and technological development centers, despite those centers being remote from major cities. It is also clear that the agencies are not content with setting up isolated offices but, rather, are working to establish a common space for working with civil stakeholders. And in the spirit of agile approaches, both the agencies and the civil actors are not waiting for these new projects to be completed before beginning work to promote collaborations, including in the field of education and training.

PRIVATE PARTIES CARRYING OUT
INTELLIGENCE INVESTIGATIONS

Another interesting phenomenon that illustrates the blurring of boundaries between the world of classified intelligence and the public is a new trend in which private parties, such as journalists, not-for-profit organizations, and even individuals, are carrying out intelligence investigations. Journalistic investigations are, of course, nothing new, nor is media coverage of issues pertaining to national security, including clandestine operations. One of the most memorable examples is the press conference Dubai Police Chief Dhahi Khalfan Tamim held following the assassination of Hamas operative Mahmoud al-Mabhouh in 2010, in which Tamim presented the results of an investigation that suggested that the Mossad was behind the assassination.[9] But in recent years it appears that not only are civil-led investigations more numerous and in-depth, but they are increasingly using intelligence practices in a way that would shame the best of intelligence organizations.

Of course, the main reason for this trend is the abundance of visible, quality information that is publicly available. At the same time, modern information technologies enable virtual networks of people, from different fields and with different expertise but with a common agenda, to reveal events that could threaten the public peace. The growing public demand for transparency, as well as the media's desire to present facts and fight concealment and disinformation efforts carried out by state-led organizations, all give impetus to such initiatives. Investigators from the field of cyber security are particularly inspired, having for years investigated cyber-attacks using information that is mostly held by civilians, to improve collective security capabilities and expose attackers.[10]

The investigations are not only carried out by media outlets, but also by private companies, groups, and individuals. For example, the Bellingcat collective of researchers, which published the investigation into the attempted assassination of Alexei Navalny, a Russian opposition leader, has been operating since 2014 and includes several full-time volunteer researchers who specialize in extracting open-source intelligence (OSINT). They focus on security incidents, crime, and human rights violations. Another example is the website Forensic Architecture, which in 2021 published a comprehensive forensic investigation into the explosion in the port of Beirut. The site belongs to a civilian research institute operating from London and investigating human rights violations.[11] A third case is the Canadian Citizen Lab, an academic laboratory that in mid-2021 published a comprehensive study on the involvement of the Israeli offensive cyber company NSO in the monitoring of human rights activists, journalists, and politicians.

It is interesting to note that in those three cases, the researchers sometimes describe the sources of information and the research methodologies used.[12] The investigation into the attempted assassination of Navalny is a good example of this: the publication detailed, among other things, characteristics of the information black market in Russia, a variety of assumptions that the researchers relied upon, and screenshots of information sources used. In another case, a group of students published the methodology and information sources they used in attempting to locate ISIS leader Abu Bakr al-Baghdadi.[13]

It is not surprising that these investigations are based on information drawn from a variety of different sources—some legal and some less so, with significant use of crowdsourcing (see chapter 7). John Scott-Railton, who investigated, among other things, the events of the storming of the U.S. Capitol and NSO's exploits, addressed his questions to the public through his Twitter account.[14] The Bellingcat website used data it acquired through the darknet, including telephone contacts, locations, flights, vehicles, IDs, and so on, to discover the identities of the Navalny assassins. Forensic Architecture's Beirut explosion analysis relied on unique forensic operations, including video footage analysis from the scene of the incident and an estimation of the type and quantity of explosives in the warehouse based on the pattern of the blast and its destruction.

Such examples will proliferate in the coming years, and intelligence organizations should take notice of the phenomenon. These investigations present an advanced approach to the use of a variety of sources, the great potential inherent in open or semi-open information, and the power inherent in crowdsourcing. They have the potential to bolster the power of intelligence organizations, especially by improving access to arenas that are less accessible or less known to the agencies.[15]

These cases all illustrate the blurring boundaries between passive data collection, active information retrieval, research, and action based on intelligence insights. In other words, these cases are another example of the diminished relevance of the traditional concept of the intelligence cycle, even though (and maybe because) they are carried out outside the rigid organizational context of intelligence services. On the other hand, these investigations should constitute a warning sign for the services: they must operate under the assumption that a significant proportion of their activities—especially those that will, by design or otherwise, resonate with the public—will be investigated at a high level by stakeholders, adversaries, and others and may even become the subject of exposés or disinformation campaigns.

PRIVATIZATION OF INTELLIGENCE ACTIVITIES

The privatization of government activities to contractors to carry out security-related operations is not a new phenomenon.[16] Outsourcing is a practice designed to increase the efficiency of the organization, reduce costs, and allow the organization to focus on the core activities in which it excels.

The events of 9/11 and the emergence of cyber as an offensive and defensive field, in tandem with cuts to the defense budget with flow-on effects of cuts to research and development and manpower budgets, have accelerated the trend.[17] Further, the fact that technological innovations, especially in the field of information technology, are led by the civil sector gives the private market an advantage over the public sector.[18]

This privatization trend has not skipped over intelligence services and operations, particularly—but not only—in the cyber realm. Research and development, cyber and general operations, information collection and processing—all are already carried out by private companies for security and intelligence services. Here, too, the main consideration is efficiency and cost reduction. Intelligence organizations have been operating in a reality of budget constraints in recent decades; they are in competition with private companies for human resources and lack skilled manpower. As such, they must find other solutions to achieve their set tasks.

The situation in which the American IC found itself following the fall of the Communist bloc set the scene for its outsourcing. Immediately following the collapse, the huge intelligence system built to deal with the former global powerhouse had to undergo dramatic cuts, including layoffs, with significant pension payouts. The budget and manpower cuts to American intelligence agencies in 1997–2002 amounted to about 25 percent of the workforce, with the CIA alone losing about 16 percent of its manpower.[19] But it soon became clear that in place of the major threat that was no longer, small threats were emerging, including terrorism, crime, and ethnic conflicts.[20] In such conditions, the U.S. services had no choice but to outsource some of the intelligence activities, including sensitive ones.

At the same time, the intelligence services realized that if they wanted to maintain a technological advantage over their adversaries, they had to adopt advanced technologies from the private market. They no longer had a monopoly on information and knowledge in general, and this change revealed the power of open-source information produced and collected by large companies, particularly big tech. The agencies, therefore, understood that they had to take advantage of the private market, even if it meant privatizing operations and assets that the intelligence profession until that time had considered sacred.

There is another motivation for the outsourcing of offensive cyber operations, including cyber espionage. As noted earlier, this type of activity makes it difficult to attribute the attack to a specific actor, state or otherwise. Even when the IP address of the attacking or collecting entity is discovered, it is difficult to pinpoint the specific entity, as computers can be hacked and taken over remotely with or without the owner's knowledge. In cyberspace there is also the ability to cover or erase traces of the attacker or collector, and to destroy or plant fabricated evidence. Transferring the execution of cyber operations to private actors makes it even more difficult to attribute the attack to a state entity and lowers the chance of counteraction by the attacked.

Under these conditions, a market of "private intelligence organizations" that provide services to intelligence agencies has been established. Data on the extent of the phenomenon in the American ICs is classified, but in 2007 it was reported that 70 percent of the U.S. intelligence budget was allocated to private companies. That same year, a former CIA executive estimated that contractors make up about 50 to 60 percent of the CIA's workforce.[21] And in 2009, it was reported that more than 50 percent of the DIA's manpower was made up of outside contractors.[22]

This trend creates a significant challenge for intelligence organizations.

First, a kind of vicious cycle has arisen in which quality personnel leave the agencies with the aim of rejoining them as contractors with better pay and conditions, which in turn exacerbates the agencies' manpower problem.

Second, it is more difficult for regulatory bodies to monitor the legality of intelligence operations when they are carried out by private entities.

Third, tenders for outsourcing intelligence missions are often not made public, which impairs not only oversight over engagement of companies, but also impacts the potential for competition between relevant companies. In this context, the security clearance problem should be noted: issuing a security clearance to a new employee, and certainly a contractor, is a long and tedious process that sometimes does not meet the needs of the agencies.

In such conditions, former employees with a security clearance have an advantage, and it is not surprising that they are "snatched up" by the large corporations, especially the big defense contractors. The problem is so acute that in 2016, about 80 percent of the forty-five thousand contractor employees in the intelligence field in the United States belonged to five big-tech corporations.[23] Moreover, in 2007, a contractor employee cost the taxpayer twice as much as each federally employed counterpart.[24]

Fourth is the standing incentive that drives companies, which is essentially a commercial incentive, as they are obligated to show profits to shareholders. When a commercial interest meets a situation of lack of transparency and lack of competition, the intelligence product itself may be impaired.

Last, as the Snowden affair has shown, contracted employees may be a more likely source of sensitive information leakage.[25]

Despite these challenges, it is worth remembering that the phenomenon of "private intelligence organizations" has emerged as a response to real need and difficulties. Thus, intelligence services must find ways to deal with the aforementioned challenges. First and foremost, decision makers need to manage the delicate balance between tasks performed in-house and those transferred to private hands. Among the considerations are issues related to the close supervision of contractors engaged in sensitive tasks, including in-depth background checks. Second, the use of products from companies affiliated with rival governments and involved in illegal activities should be avoided. Last, intelligence organizations must assume that information leaks will occur and, therefore, must be as prepared as possible—both to allow detection ahead of time and to deal with potential repercussions from the moment the leaks are discovered.

INTELLIGENCE AND PUBLIC RELATIONS

The revelation regarding the U.S. intelligence community's use of big technology companies' databases, in the wake of the Snowden affair, has led to a widespread public trust crisis. It has also led to ethical questions about the tension between the public's right to privacy and its security, and the ethical obligation of the intelligence community to be transparent in its use of private information. True, as former president Obama said, "You can't have 100-percent security and also have 100-percent privacy."[26] At the same time, in democratic regimes, the use of intellectual property and private information, and any invasion of privacy, require transparency and cooperation with the public.

Until a few years ago, most communication between intelligence communities and the public was one-sided and revolved around a limited supply of information and assessments regarding different types of threats. This perception is changing now: the public is demanding more transparency, it is showing more interest in security challenges, and it is much more critical of decision makers. Intelligence organizations, therefore, cannot continue to operate in the dark and must allow the public to evaluate elected officials' policies on national security issues, including by making intelligence products accessible. This issue is becoming increasingly important in the face of the struggle for consciousness in the post-truth age. Part of the state's obligation to its citizens is to create certainty and prevent disinformation. In such conditions, exchange between the intelligence agencies and the public is doubly important.[27]

In this case, too, American services are leading the trend of opening up to the public. In addition to the oversight by House of Representatives and Senate committees, intelligence agencies are sharing intelligence and methodological information as part of a transparency policy pursued over the past decade. The then-head of the DNI, James Clapper, decided, following the Snowden affair and on the orders of President Obama, to promote an orderly policy to bolster transparency by sharing with the public both information on what the intelligence community does with the information it collects and national intelligence assessments.[28]

The Office of the National Intelligence Director's work plan includes a series of principles for ensuring that the work of the intelligence community is transparent to the public: sharing the manner in which it works and the legal foundation for its work; making available some of the national intelligence products in matters of national or economic interest; and regulating the mechanisms and officials that are required to implement the policy.[29] The director of National Intelligence has established an Office of Civil Intelligence and a

Liberties, Privacy and Transparency Council, which meets twice a quarter to review policy implementation and formulate a work plan.

Several collaborative projects are noteworthy here:

- The FBI collaborates with more than four hundred companies involved in national critical infrastructure through an organization called INFRAGARD. It shares intelligence assessments and concrete threats with companies and organizations in real time, receives information from the private sector, and releases to the public various reports—on crime at the national level, as well as analyses, including methods of investigations, psychological analyses, and so forth.[30]
- The NSA distributes reports on the private sector cyber defense strategy.
- The CIA publishes articles written by current and retired intelligence professionals for the benefit of the intelligence community and the general public, together with an encyclopedia that includes historical information on global intelligence, terrorism, and international relations developments.
- The U.S. Indopacific Command, which deals with the Chinese challenge, publicizes information about Chinese policy in the region. The purpose is to inform businesspeople and thus harness the public to act in such a way that blocks business moves led by the Chinese government.
- The DIA is keeping up—it publishes in-depth academic analyses of U.S. rivals' (e.g., Iran, Russia, and China) security policies and military and intelligence capabilities.[31]

Collaborations with the public also take place through technology companies, with one of the most prominent being around election security. In the United States and beyond, intelligence communities are educating private and public companies and organizations about cyber threats, particularly those related to the democratic election process. For example, the FITF (Foreign Influence Task Force) established in 2017 by the FBI to identify and deal with foreign influence attempts in the United States, regularly briefs private companies, including on classified information. The companies, for their part, particularly technology and cyber companies, hold significant knowledge of strategic and concrete threats, and thus share information with the community.

Intelligence organizations seeking to open up to the public face significant challenges and barriers: The culture of secrecy within the agencies leads to their perception that the public space is an unclassified arena where intelligence issues should not be discussed. Integrating the unclassified public space and the intelligence community's classified spheres is foreign and unnatural to intelligence personnel. Publicly releasing intelligence products and information about intelligence activities and assets also exposes them to adversaries, who can then use those products to uncover sources, practices, and other assets—and even act to mislead the intelligence community. And yet, intelligence communities must provide the public with the opportunity to know and understand the system and conditions under which the state operates, including external and internal threats. They should, if possible, provide more strategic and specific warnings and report on the future intentions of enemy actors and the expected consequences.

Chapter 7

Intelligence and Civic Engagement

Emphasizing Collaboration

One of the devastating consequences of President Trump's four years in office is that public confidence in the American intelligence system was significantly undermined. For the sake of fairness, it should be noted that this outcome was partly the result of a broader process of waning trust in traditional knowledge institutions, including academia and public health—undoubtedly a characteristic of the zeitgeist of the information age. Restoring trust in the intelligence establishment is, therefore, a task of paramount importance in democratic regimes. In breaking down the boundaries of intelligence systems and encouraging the public to contribute to the intelligence enterprise at the national level, new channels of mutual trust will be created. But, no less important, opening intelligence systems to the public entails several additional benefits to the organizations themselves:

- First, it will allow a faster transfer of knowledge and its derivatives (e.g., human resources) from the private to the public sector, which will multiply the innovation capability of intelligence organizations.
- Second, it will allow intelligence organizations to refine and diversify their outputs, as they will not have to rely only on a relatively limited pool of internal resources.
- Third, it will provide intelligence organizations with additional perspectives, which are by nature created outside the intelligence bubble.

Achieving these goals requires no less than a paradigmatic revolution in the way intelligence organizations perceive themselves in relation to the public.

This chapter presents a conceptual framework for how intelligence organizations can collaborate with the public. I will introduce two concepts:

1. The first is based on the principle of crowdsourcing and how it can be integrated into intelligence work, to create a new intelligence discipline that I call CROSINT.
2. The second concept, prosumer, refers to a conceptual framework for the integration of individual citizens in intelligence work.

These two concepts complement each other and present a decentralized and hybrid approach to conducting intelligence: One refers to the public as a community; the other refers to individuals within that community. It should be emphasized that I consciously choose not to engage extensively with the ethical aspects of integrating the public into intelligence work, with issues of privacy, or with the danger of transferring domains that are meant to be held by the state to private actors. Some of these problems were discussed in the previous chapter, but in general they require an in-depth discussion that is beyond the scope of this work.

CROSINT: A NEW INTELLIGENCE DISCIPLINE[1]

The term crowdsourcing refers to a wide range of situations in which ideas, opinions, or any other product is produced by a large group of people.[2] A more precise definition refers to a model based on information technology (IT), intended for problem solving, idea creation, and manufacturing, which leverages scattered knowledge from groups and individuals to generate diverse resources for organizations.[3] In other words, crowdsourcing—as a concept of knowledge development through information technology—strives to combine central efficiency and control (in the same vein as traditional approaches to research and strategic planning) with the added benefit of democratizing and decentralizing innovation and creativity.

One relevant subset of crowdsourcing is online communities of experts or online communities of practice. In such communities, which usually revolve around a specific field (such as marketing, design, etc.), experts share specialized knowledge with their colleagues, usually about analytical tasks, such as conducting research or forecasting, or implementing ideas proposed by a general audience.

The use of crowdsourcing for policy formulation and implementation spread widely after it gained a foothold in the business world. To a large extent, the growth of crowdsourcing can be attributed to the public's dissatisfaction with policy outcomes and an expectation that crowds might achieve better results.[4] Political crises, the rise of populist parties and forces, the decline of the political center, and the apparent lack of predictability (and understanding) of election results have led many to question traditional political processes and seek new methods—not necessarily to replace traditional policy-making and implementation methods, but to work in combination with them. Indeed, many projects around the world seek to involve the public in policy planning processes at various government levels (state, municipal). Crowdsourcing projects involve developing legislation and regulation; learning about public preferences and needs; crisis responses; direct communication between elected officials, state institutions, and the public itself; and even replacing traditional polling methods, with the aim of better forecasting political election results.

Crowdsourcing also plays a special role in the formulation and implementation of national security policies. The growing proliferation of IT not only poses challenges to national security, but also expands the potential for effective responses to rising threats. For those tasked with protecting national security, IT also offers a space where the public can be invited to participate and contribute its capabilities and knowledge to dealing with security challenges. Examples from recent years are numerous and come from two main dimensions of action related to national security: first, data collection and interpretation, mainly for internal security needs; and, second, finding solutions—mainly technological—for security challenges.

Crowdsourcing can be a powerful tool for collecting and interpreting information in real time, especially during crises. For example, during the riots in Britain in the summer of 2011, the public uploaded pictures of rioters and looters to Flickr to assist enforcement agencies in identification. Later, law enforcement agencies launched a Twitter-based campaign to encourage the public to help to identify rioters, whether by uploading pictures or videos, or by tracking rioters' tweets.[5]

Another interesting example, involving a global crowdsourcing effort, was around the attempt to solve the mystery of the lost Malaysia Airlines Flight 370. Tremendous effort and resources were put into finding the airplane's remains, including cutting-edge scanning and mapping technology.

Along with ships and aircraft from Australia, China, India, Japan, Malaysia, New Zealand, South Korea, the United Kingdom, and the United States, another method was used—crowdsourcing. Because mechanically analyzing vast oceanic spaces would have taken too long, satellite images were made available to the general public by Tomnod (a project owned by Colorado-based satellite company DigitalGlobe) so it could help with the search.

Finding technological solutions to security challenges is the second common use case for crowdsourcing. R&D bodies—primarily in the English-speaking world—have been using crowdsourcing to find solutions (mainly technological) for security problems. DARPA, for example, has promoted a number of initiatives in this vein. In 2009, it offered a $40,000 prize to anyone who could develop an efficient system to locate thousands of balloons around the United States (the Red Balloon Challenge). The winner was an MIT group that used social media-based crowdsourcing to locate the balloons.[6]

In 2011, DARPA challenged researchers to develop an algorithm to decode shredded documents (the shredder challenge). The organization uploaded scraps of shredded documents and invited the public to decipher them, with a $50,000 prize for the winner. Nine thousand teams took part in the project, and the winner was a group of San Francisco programmers who solved the challenge within thirty-three days.[7]

The British government, too, is experimenting with crowdsourcing. In 2011, the GCHQ launched a competition called CanyouCrackit ("Can You Crack It?") to identify experts from among the public who could crack sophisticated codes. The participants were challenged to crack codes on well-encrypted documents, and the GCHQ attempted to recruit the winners.[8]

Finally, in early February 2017, the U.S. Intelligence and Advanced Research Projects Activity (IARPA) announced the launch of the CREATE project. The project aims to improve analytical reasoning and communication of analytical reasoning to consumers and partners of the intelligence community through crowdsourcing. The American intelligence community has long grappled with the challenge of improving its analytical and theoretical capabilities and, to that end, has established various research programs under the umbrella term structured analytic techniques (SATs). These techniques provide a set of analytical tools for intelligence researchers, but they do not encourage cooperation and codevelopment of knowledge by researchers. Rather, they are "recipes" for research, intended for the individual researcher or small groups of researchers. The CREATE project is designed to address the limitations of existing methodologies by developing technological capabilities that support analysis based on the principles of collaboration and crowdsourcing. The assumption underlying the project is that experts from a variety of fields, who are not necessarily intelligence personnel or members of the intelligence community, can develop knowledge that will challenge researchers in the intelligence field. This process can help prevent many inherent problems of research, including cognitive biases.

The increasing popularity of crowdsourcing, including for applications in the world of intelligence and law enforcement, together with profound changes in intelligence productivity, has led some to speculate on the extent to which crowdsourcing is an intelligence discipline, alongside the five "traditional" disciplines (SIGINT, HUMINT, GEOINT, OSINT, MASINT).[9]

The question that arises in this context is whether crowdsourcing is an extension of other disciplines, such as HUMINT or OSINT, or a discipline in its own right. Like Stottlemyre, I believe that it is a unique discipline that does not fully overlap with any other discipline: it does not include a dimension of secrecy (whether in the form of collection or the type of information obtained) and is not limited to "one-on-one" (agent versus operator) interactions, as does human intelligence in its classic form. Crowdsourcing also does not exactly conform to the principles of OSINT, which assume, among other things, that the data collection is passive (i.e., the information comes from a source that is independent from the collection process and is "waiting" to be collected). This new discipline, to which I shall refer here as crowdsourced intelligence (CROSINT), combines the human dimension of HUMINT and the visible dimension of OSINT but involves approaching many people broadly, publicly—not covertly—to provide information that is sensitive but not classified.

Crowdsourcing's success has ignited great hopes that using its methodologies will help intelligence organizations overcome the challenges of collecting, processing, assessing, and forecasting information, both on the tactical level (e.g., dealing with terrorist attacks) and on the strategic level (e.g., forecasting revolutions or election results). Crowdsourcing can also assist in overcoming three basic challenges of intelligence activity: individual and group cognitive failures, pathologies resulting from organizational structures and work processes, and the inescapable complexity of the operational and strategic environment.

The cognitive challenge, one set of challenges in strategic planning, stems from individual and group cognitive limitations.[10] Human perception is an active process, in which the individual and the group construct a version of reality based on assumptions and concepts. However, this process is awash with cognitive biases and generally does not have an internal cognitive mechanism to account for the basic assumptions and conditions that shape it.[11]

The organizational challenge relates to organizational structures, procedures, and behaviors. In general, these challenges can be characterized as problems in organizational communication. These problems lead to a lack of information sharing and knowledge development, which can create a strategic threat to organizations as different functions are often supported by different information sources, all of which are needed to develop the strategic knowledge that underlies planning and decision making.

The challenge of the strategic environment relates to key characteristics of the operational and strategic environment in which organizations operate: great complexity and the rapid pace of internal changes. This has several implications:

- First, the cognitive ability of individuals and groups to contain such complexity is limited.

- Second, the rate of change often does not allow for orderly planning and decision-making processes but, rather, requires urgent and ongoing attention.
- Third, it is difficult to identify a direct link between action and outcome, and to forecast the impact of a given process or action.

The use of large communities (or crowds) partially overcomes the complexity and cognitive challenges in intelligence activity, because the collective mind is far more powerful and varied than the individual. Large groups can collect vast and varied amounts of information, work relatively well and rapidly, and analyze it from a variety of perspectives, which collectively reduces—but does not prevent—conceptual distortions. The establishment of a crowdsourcing community to accompany the organization (and to which members of the organization are invited to join and contribute their knowledge) improves organizational communication. Finally, the online nature of these communities and their global circulation, coupled with the fact that usually they are not financially motivated, enable complex intelligence operations to be carried out simply, efficiently, rapidly, and inexpensively.[12]

Above all, crowdsourcing enables intelligence personnel to diversify their points of view when they examine a given subject of research. The essence of crowdsourcing is the bringing together of many people, from different backgrounds, with different personalities, different behavioral and intellectual characteristics, and from many different fields. This range enables a more complex analysis, which combines a variety of points of view that usually are not available to a small team of researchers, all in a relatively short period of time and at relatively low costs when compared to potential outcomes.[13] This is all the more significant when it comes to virtual platforms on which hundreds, even thousands, of people collaborate in real time. The fact that crowd-based discourse is decentralized rather than structured hierarchically or organizationally allows interesting internal dynamics to develop, which have analytical value in their own right. Finally, the connection between a closed group (such as the intelligence community) and an open group (such as the crowdsourced community) redefines and expands the boundaries of the intelligence community.

Nevertheless, it would be an error to view crowdsourcing as a complete solution to all the data collection and research challenges that intelligence organizations face. The method does present several problems: studies have shown that for certain types of problems, crowdsourcing is not necessarily effective and may produce less accurate results than those of individuals or small groups of researchers. This is partly due to the fact that crowd-based experiences tend to be less structured than the research methodologies that the intelligence community traditionally accepts. In addition, it is difficult for participants to identify and focus on the right or useful insights within a very wide range of operations; frequently, there is confusion between opinion and information, general knowledge and accurate empirical facts. In this way, crowdsourcing may not meet the strict methodological standards that intelligence organizations typically use.

Problems are also inherent in relying on a broad group of participants, some of whom are not experts and whose motives for participation are not always clear. In some cases, due to lack of professionalism or misunderstanding of the research question (e.g., in cases where the initiating organization seeks to conceal aspects of the research, such as its identity or other sensitive facts), irrelevant information generated through the crowdsourcing activity may overshadow the valuable information that is produced.

Finally, depending on the nature of the problem, crowd-based analysis may not always be the appropriate methodology. Intelligence organizations occasionally address problems that can be solved only through the acquisition of sensitive information, which the public does not have a relative advantage in obtaining or analyzing. In other cases, addressing or analyzing the problem requires divulging secret information that the organization seeks to protect; in such cases, an open discussion involving wide audiences might be a security threat. Indeed, one of the main arguments against crowdsourcing by intelligence organizations is the lack of secrecy inherent in the process.

However, on the strategic level (and in certain respects, on the tactical level) intelligence challenges are not always secret (although the data on which assessments are based may be classified). Often, especially in knowledge development, the task is not related to information at all but to cognitive processes, knowledge development, and knowledge itself. Intelligence organizations may be hesitant to publicize certain issues of interest, but the use of open platforms in which ordinary people participate does not necessarily entail a risk of exposing sensitive information. When an intelligence organization poses a question to the public, it has no need to disclose all the layers of the question, let alone the classified ones. Moreover, in comparison to social networks (where the personal profile or username is visible to all), many crowdsourcing platforms allow users to hide their identity (e.g., by participating anonymously), build areas that are restricted to a certain audience, and generally restrict access to the platform by requiring a username and password.

Looking into the future, interesting and promising developments in crowdsourcing are highly relevant for intelligence organizations. The field is developing in new directions, including medicine and higher education—two areas that have been slow to adopt the methodology but are increasingly doing so with great enthusiasm. Efforts are also being made to find new incentive mechanisms to motivate people who are part of large communities to actively contribute to them. Another direction is the development of multidimensional, real-time graphical representations of knowledge, insights, patterns, biases, and blind spots of crowd-based discourse.

The key direction for development in the field lies in bringing together people and machines; more precisely, the use of advanced technologies, especially AI, for the analysis of crowdsourced discourse and the use of crowds to enhance AI capabilities, particularly machine learning. These two directions can lead to what I call Big Knowledge: the aggregate knowledge of communities and second-order insights that can be derived from discourse analysis (i.e., who says what and why), along with the use of knowledge developed by human communities to strengthen machine capabilities in knowledge development.

Interestingly, the next generation of crowdsourcing has arrived at the intelligence community: Unanimous AI launched new software designed to generate forecasts and insights through crowdsourcing. The system on which the software is based is called "swarm intelligence" and is distinguished from traditional crowdsourcing in that it synchronizes the crowd's insights and analyzes the interactions between them in real time. According to the company's CEO, it is possible to make group decisions on the basis of the "competition" between the participants at any time, in real time, using machine learning to help the community members learn about the positions of their colleagues and quickly refine their insights and forecasts.[14]

Already at the end of 2016, IARPA launched the hybrid forecasting competition (HFC), whose goal is to examine whether human–machine interfaces can improve the forecasting of geopolitical events. IARPA encourages the public to register for the program and participate in the forecasts while providing an online interface that includes a variety of technological applications.[15]

Crowdsourcing is not a universal solution to the challenges that intelligence organizations face, but the judicious and varied use of available tools at every stage of policy formulation and intelligence can yield beneficial results. Crowdsourced intelligence organizations will change the way they operate, particularly with respect to operation and compartmentalization, to redefine the nature and tasks associated with data collection and research, and to redefine the concept of secrecy and protection of organizational data. Investing in tools that combine advanced technological platforms with the ability to decentralize the processes of data collection and knowledge production—a central aspect of the CROSINT discipline—will undoubtedly give intelligence organizations a competitive advantage.

PROSUMER[16]

In 1980, futurist Alvin Toffler coined the word "prosumer" to describe a new form of interactions and outcomes between the traditional producers and consumers.[17] Only a decade and a half later, this concept became common, with the shift from a linear and stable to a nonlinear dynamic mode of exchange, in which consumers are involved in the acts of production, marketing, distribution, and advertisement.[18]

In the world of business, the idea of cocreation of value initially marked the need to integrate consumers in the acts of development, production, marketing, and advertising, rather than the act of consumption alone. Trends related to changes in consumer behavior, as well as the development of IT technologies, demonstrated to producers the need—and the potential—in moving consumers from the realm of consumption into new domains.[19] Relinquishing absolute control over certain elements in the process of production, traditionally exclusively in the hands of producers, was aimed at improving and adjusting the fashion in which industries operate in a new and changing world.

In the last decade, the concept of the prosumer, initially discussed in the fields of business and economics, has been gaining much popularity in the fields of humanities and social studies. The focal point here is the participation of individuals and collectives in the production of political power—most commonly in political campaigns. In this respect, one might regard the political campaign as a process aimed at producing a "product," which is itself an expression or manifestation of political power (e.g., election to a political position, legislation, etc.). The political involvement of individuals and groups in campaigns, for example, by expressing opinions in social media, can be described in terms of prosumption, as it is very similar to consumers' involvement in the act of production: participants create political content and conduct political activity, which, in turn, is supposed to create a political outcome (i.e., a political product) in the light of guidelines that politicians determine.

Yet, this description does not relate to the state as the starting point or the relations between the state and its citizens. The idea of prosumption should, therefore, be expanded to a domain in which the state itself, as a political actor, is the producer and its citizens are the consumers. In this light, prosumption should be perceived as acts conducted by citizens who operate in order to fulfill aims (i.e., produce products), which had traditionally been within the sole purview of the state.

To shed light on this idea, we must expand the scope of the meaning of prosumption to the political sphere and create an analogy between the sphere of business and economics and the political one. By using this analogy, I shall address the state (or its apparatuses) as a producer, the citizen as a consumer, and the public good or service as the product. In the context of this book, national security is a public good because once provided, it is difficult to exclude people within the country from the safety and security generated, and multiple individuals can enjoy the added safety and security without limiting that received by others.[20]

Let us address the state as a producer that produces a "public good" for the benefit of the community. The public good is produced for the state's citizens, and in this respect, we can identify the latter as consumers. It is true that the citizens operate within the framework of the state, and one might claim that every citizen by definition is both a producer and a consumer. Take, for example, models of regular armies based on compulsory enlistment (such as the Israeli Defense Force): the purpose of the army is to defend the nation (i.e., to provide a public good, which is national security). One might claim that because these armies are composed of enlisted citizens, the latter are prosumers: they take part both in production and in consumption of the public good. However, when I make the analogy of the state as the producer and its citizens as consumers, it is an analogy that lies within the realm of social structures, not from the perspective of the agents operating within those structures. Indeed, citizens operate within the state's organizational framework; but when I address the state as a producer, I refer to the structures or the organizations that produce the public good, not to the individuals who operate within them. It is clear, of course, that these state organizations are composed of individuals, yet one must distinguish an organization composed of individuals (I would define them as producers) from individuals operating outside these organizations (I would define them as consumers). Similarly, companies are composed of individuals, yet structurally described as producers—even though under certain circumstances, these individuals themselves are consumers of their own products.

We can demonstrate this idea using as an example the use of force by the state. An elementary principle defines the idea of state sovereignty as its monopoly on the use of force and violence within a given territory.[21] For example, military operations are conducted in the name of the state and by organizations sanctioned within the framework of the state—even when operating under cover. The public good (product) in this case is what the state defines as its strategic goal in carrying out this military operation—for example, providing its citizens (i.e., consumers) with security.

The availability of technology and information allows individuals and groups to participate in production of the public good. Again, we must not confuse this kind of participation with actions that individuals conduct in the name of the state and through its own apparatuses (e.g., spies, special ops, or even military units). When arguing that individuals and groups can participate in the production of a public good related to the use of violent means, I mean participation not necessarily organized by the state, even if in some respects the state might condone or influence such activities.

There are many examples, and I shall briefly present one, although outdated, that still demonstrates my argument nicely: "Mrs. Galt" was an American housewife and a mother during the day, and a self-appointed spy-master at night. In 2002–2003, she infiltrated "unpublicized websites that al-Qaeda and other terror groups used for their routine communications and sweet-talked her interlocutors into revealing their plans, often with fatal consequences for the terrorists."[22]

Therefore, we can identify two types of prosumers within the national security domain (and the political sphere in general), both expressions of voluntary political activity by individuals or groups:

1. The first is related to prosumerist political participation, which is not established by the state but, rather, as an independent venture or under the guidance of a political figure or entity.
2. The second is related to prosumerist participaton, which is indirectly supported by the state and yields (or from another perspective— expands) its traditional authority. It can be described as decentralization of some of the state's responsibilities, delivering them directly to its citizens.

Chapter 8

TEMPINT

A New Intelligence Paradigm

The new age of intelligence requires the formulation of new concepts for the regulation of intelligence. The powerful but outdated concept of the intelligence cycle expresses a logic like an industrial production line, which views intelligence work as divided into separate components, each a separate organizational function (collection, processing, research, distribution, guidance) and independent but interacting with the other components at defined junctures. The idea of the intelligence cycle sees intelligence as a closed manufacturing system that makes periodic contact with external actors, especially decision makers, and sees them as passive consumers supplied with the intelligence product in a one-way process: intelligence organizations produce intelligence products, transfer them to consumers, who in turn give feedback to the organization, which is supposed to adopt the feedback and adapt its work accordingly.

However, in recent years this concept has experienced a change. The understanding that the present era embodies a real revolution in intelligence matters, not just changes and adjustments to the way intelligence organizations operate and are built, also promotes attempts to conceptualize a new intelligence process. In the following lines I will briefly review several (relatively) new alternative concepts to the intelligence cycle: activity-based intelligence (ABI) and object-based production. I will then describe a new concept that—together with Dr. Roey Tzezana—I've dubbed temporal intelligence (TEMPINT). It isn't my intention to provide a fully detailed description of these approaches, but merely to preview approaches that challenge the traditional concept of the intelligence cycle.

Activity-based intelligence is a concept created from the accumulated American experience of identifying targets for special operations. At its core, it is a multidisciplinary intelligence approach to activity-based data analysis to "resolve unknown-unknowns, develop intelligence, and drive collection."[1]

The intelligence methods that the army implemented in Afghanistan and Iraq revealed how much the intelligence cycle approach is irrelevant to the challenges that intelligence services face. On the other hand, the idea of ABI has produced impressive successes in exposing terrorist networks in those countries.

The linear conception of the intelligence cycle began by identifying the terrorist as a collection target, but in practice it was difficult to identify the terrorists from among the general population. Thus, American analysts began integrating data gathered from a variety of sensors, combined with geographic data. Often, the only thing common among the various data sets being collected was the metadata about time and location. As such, they were forced to develop analytical methodologies to extract insights and patterns from large and diverse databases. These databases were called activities: events and transactions between entities (e.g., people or vehicles) in a given area. Sometimes, analysts discovered a series of unconventional events that matched each other in different database scales; when the events were intersected, the path of the entity they were following came into focus. From that point, gathering data about the newly discovered target, analyzing the data, and forecasting behavior based on patterns discovered in its "life cycle" created a new range of intelligence products that were much more useful than had been produced using previous methodologies. That is how the ABI got its name.

As Gregory F. Treverton argues, unlike the concept of the intelligence cycle, activity-based intelligence does not assume that intelligence agents know what they are looking for. This concept does not assume linearity but, rather, is based on a neutral sequence of events, some connected to one another and others not. Traditional intelligence gives priority to the collection: when analysis reveals an intelligence gap, the first response of intelligence personnel is to gather more data to fill the gap. However, according to Treverton, the world is full of data, and activity-based intelligence reminds us that the problem is not in the data. Thus, although the intelligence cycle paradigm provides a place of honor for the collection and its secret sources, for activity-based intelligence, all data are neutral and are mostly facts. No sources are "reliable" or "dubious"; data become "good" or "bad" only when they stand in relation to other data and only when they provide actionable insights, such as target location or decryption of a terrorist network.

In the words of then-head of the National Geospatial Agency (NGA) Letitia A. Long, "We are being challenged to think in terms of activity-based GEOINT rather than target-based GEOINT and to explain not only where something is happening, but also why. Contextual GEOINT is what is now required."[2]

And elsewhere:

"[Activity-based intelligence is] . . . a high-quality methodology for maximizing the value we can derive from "Big Data . . . " That is, making the new discoveries about adversary patterns and networks that give two crucial advantages—unique insights and more decision space—to policy makers, military planners and operators, intelligence analysts, law enforcement and first responders.

The most complete discussion of ABI was produced by Patrick Biltgen and Stephen Ryan in the book *Activity-Based Intelligence: Principles and Applications*.[3] The two define it as a "set of spatiotemporal analytic methods to discover correlations, resolve unknowns, understand networks, develop knowledge and drive collection using diverse multi-INT data sets." The two define four central axes of the approach:

1. Georeference to discover: Use data from the same time and place to identify events or entities.
2. Sequence neutrality: Understanding that sometimes a piece of the puzzle can be found before understanding that there is a puzzle to be put together.
3. Data neutrality: The assumption that data is not "good" or "bad" per se; it can be relevant regardless of its origin—it all depends on the context in which the data is used.
4. Integration before exploitation: The ability to quickly create correlations between data, because fragments of data can take on greater meaning when they are combined than when separate.

A somewhat related concept is object-based production (OBP)[4]—the production of intelligence, based on an object or an interest. This approach assumes that intelligence has a basic problem of inadequate organization of existing data and that a better, more efficient organizational structure is required. Proponents of OBP argue that intelligence reports should be based on data generated from various types of knowledge and organizational functions; and that intelligence products should be distributed with a focus on the object being investigated, rather than according to the traditional linear model. OBP principles result in intelligence being produced as one object-centric model; it is made available to the consumer through integration and management at the organizational level, rather than the individual product level.

The American IC has been implementing the OBP approach through the "Quellfire" project, through which it has shown that it can produce intelligence products quickly and highly effectively. It should be noted that these processes are suitable for cloud architecture, as they are inherently network-based and enable the creation of intelligence by various stakeholders, each of which has a different role at different stages of the production process. Object-based analysis enables analysts to more accurately model the real world in the way humans naturally interact with it.

Temporal intelligence (TEMPINT) was developed by the futurist Dr. Roey Tzezana, together with the author of this book.[5] In an age in which the Internet of Things (IoT) is growing in popularity, the means of collection and monitoring available to intelligence services are becoming increasingly sophisticated. James Clapper, the former U.S. director of national intelligence, stated in 2016 that the country's intelligence agencies would likely use the Internet of Things for "identification, surveillance, monitoring, location tracking, and targeting for recruitment, or to gain access to networks or user credentials."[6] Although this approach shows that the U.S. intelligence community is taking heed of this new technology, the new powers of data gathering and analysis are bound to change the current intelligence paradigms and create a new one.

In this light, TEMPINT is not a narrow intelligence collection methodology that focuses on certain sources but, rather, a new holistic approach to data collection, processing, and analysis. It is predicated on the assumption that in the not-too-distant future most people and infrastructure in the world will be subject to continuous monitoring and that the monitoring data can be collected, aggregated, and analyzed using advanced tools that will allow intelligence personnel to go back and forth in time (within the data) to develop hypotheses and perform simulations of future behavior. Figuratively, TEMPINT can be compared to a unified platform that transmits real-time information from around the world, allowing the user to focus, freeze, rewind, or forward the data snapshot, enriched with various types of data.

To illustrate the deployment of TEMPINT, consider the following scenario: An armed terrorist is assaulting shoppers in a crowded mall. He is killed within minutes and so cannot be questioned regarding his collaborators, but he has left tracks. Intelligence agencies can obtain footage of the mall security cameras to see where he entered. They can review parking lot security camera footage to identify his car. This is where the investigation often crawls to a halt, but in a future world in which the IoT is prevalent, the analysts can follow the car back in time, using the many recordings and information gleaned from cameras and sensors on the roads. In a completely wired world, analysts can essentially rewind time to identify all the people with whom the terrorist has met, then "run back time" for them as well to analyze their tracks.

This approach allows us to test new hypotheses on old data collected and stored for no real purpose at the time. In the past, intelligence agencies would have been extremely picky in data collection because of both the difficulty in obtaining data and the cost of storing large amounts of information. But now, as connected sensors become abundant, with each device streaming its data practically nonstop, the agencies only need to pick that low-hanging data and store it. As a result, these agencies gain a powerful tool: as new events occur, analysts can go back to the stored data and essentially "turn back the clock" to examine how these events came to occur. The ultimate TEMPINT platform is akin to having a video of the entire world that one could zoom into, freeze, and rewind at will complete with commentary about each individual's state of health and mind, as discerned by their wearables.

Two main technological challenges stand in the way of TEMPINT, and both are presently being solved.

The first challenge is data storage. Conducting TEMPINT means that we must store large amounts of data for future review. However, surveillance data could be stripped down to the basics: sound recordings, location and activity tracking, and snapshots taken periodically from connected surveillance cameras. In addition, as I have shown, data storage capabilities have massively improved over the past few decades, and the end to the improvement is nowhere in sight.

The second technological challenge is filtering through the immense quantity of data to find the sought-after information. This challenge is being solved by rapid improvements in AI, with neural networks gaining the ability to identify faces, objects, and even abstract concepts in pictures and videos.

Indeed, TEMPINT and other concepts (and technologies) raise concerns pertaining to privacy. Understandably, citizens are concerned about governments' growing ability to monitor ordinary people. Intelligence agencies should not ignore those fears; they need to mitigate them. For example, authorities could use AI engines to identify potential terrorists without having a human reviewing the personal details of millions of citizens. The agencies could even open some of those algorithms to public scrutiny. Such transparency will help prevent misuse of information and could add a bug detection layer that the public and watchdog organizations operate.

Indeed, changes implemented by the Obama administration allowed the NSA to share the information it gathers with the other U.S. intelligence agencies without implementing privacy protections beforehand. And so, the question is no longer whether TEMPINT will be used in the future: it's already here, albeit in a limited fashion. The will for omnipresent surveillance is strong, and although the technology is still weak (at least compared to its potential), its strength is growing. We should consider it to be a new intelligence paradigm unto itself and ponder what kind of a society its inevitable use will bring about.

Chapter 9

Intelligence in the Time of COVID-19

There seems no better phenomenon than COVID-19 to illustrate the primary arguments of this book: the speed with which the coronavirus spread surprised the world; our inability to assess the scale of the phenomenon—not only when it was still in its infancy, but in fact to this day; the role of science and medical research in national-level decision making; the need to distinguish between truth and falsehood and the challenge of fake news; the role of emerging technologies in fighting the virus; issues of privacy, human rights, and public involvement in solving the problem; how the public challenged governments; and the role that intelligence agencies can or should take in dealing with the pandemic. In short, most of the issues discussed in this book all surfaced in a dramatic fashion when COVID-19 entered our lives.

When I completed the research outline for this book in early 2019, the word "corona" overwhelmingly recalled nothing more than a beer brand, and for intelligence enthusiasts it also recalled the CIA's secret satellite project back in the late 1950s (see chapter 1). By the middle of 2021, when the writing of the book was close to completion, I realized that a work dealing with intelligence change could not help but address the COVID-19 crisis. But what began as a rather informative description of the intelligence organization's efforts—as part of the entire national effort—in fighting the virus quickly became a tumultuous arena in which all the book's issues converge. And of all the efforts of intelligence organizations in the major countries reviewed in this book, the most interesting, and most extreme, example is the Israeli experience. Therefore, I will dedicate the following pages to describing the course of events in Israel as a case study for discussing broader issues at the core of this book. But first, let us briefly review what the major intelligence agencies have contributed to the global struggle against COVID-19.

To structure the discussion, I divide the involvement of intelligence communities in the COVID-19 crisis into three distinct dimensions: The first is the strategic warning level and assessments derived from such warning, which usually lack a concrete time frame regarding the emergence of threats. The second is the operational level of epidemiological intelligence dealing with, for example, the rate of virus spread in countries or specific regions. A third dimension concerns threats directly or indirectly related to the pandemic and, in particular, cyber threats.

STRATEGIC EARLY WARNING

Throughout the years, several bodies in the American intelligence community, including the ODNI, the CIA, and the Department of Defense Intelligence, have dealt with the issue of epidemic outbreaks. The main body responsible for the early detection of an epidemic is the National Center for Medical Intelligence (NCMI), which reports to the U.S. Department of Defense (and more specifically, the DIA) and monitors epidemic outbreaks, bioterrorism, and other countries' medical capabilities.[1] Alongside the intelligence community, a large number of civilian bodies in the U.S. system that deal with public health are similarly engaged in early detection of epidemic outbreaks. They are headed by the Centers for Disease Control (CDC), which is responsible for coordination at the federal level. The CDC broadly monitors public health issues and operates its own comprehensive data collection system.

At the global level, several bodies deal with such phenomena, the principal being the World Health Organization (WHO), which does not operate its own intelligence agency but relies on the intelligence capabilities—mainly civilian—of its member states.[2]

Returning to the United States, the American intelligence community has for years warned of the threat of a global pandemic. In this sense, it has achieved one of its key tasks: namely, alerting decision makers to strategic threats, or in other words, providing decision makers with strategic warning.

And yet, it is interesting to note that former president Trump was careful to point out that COVID-19 "came out of nowhere." Again and again, he described the virus as an "invisible enemy" that no one could have detected in advance.[3] These are, of course, unfounded allegations. Ample evidence shows that for more than a decade the American intelligence community has warned decision makers about the devastating potential of just such a pandemic, repeatedly using decisive language to argue that the United States had no capacity to deal with rapidly spreading epidemics with potential dire consequences for public health and the national economy.[4]

As early as 2000, a U.S. national intelligence assessment was published that examined the potential occurrence of a global pandemic. Then, in 2004, following the outbreak of the SARS virus in China in 2002, the National

Intelligence Council (NIC) published a report (*Mapping the Global Future*) in which it warned decision makers that a potential global pandemic threatened the safety of all citizens.[5] The NIC reiterated its warning of the threat in its 2008 report (*Global Trends 2025*), especially in the chapter that presented a scenario that dealt with "the emergence of a novel, highly transmissible, and virulent human respiratory illness for which there are no adequate countermeasures."[6] In 2012, against the backdrop of the Middle East Respiratory Syndrome (MERS) outbreak in the Middle East, the NIC published another report (*Global Trends 2030: Alternative Worlds*),[7] in which a future pandemic was cited as a potential "black swan" event: that is, an unexpected, rare event, with potential for large-scale disruptive consequences.

The NIC is, of course, not the only body that raised the issue. In the American intelligence community's annual publication—*Worldwide Threat Assessment of the U.S. Intelligence Community*, which deals with the main threats facing the nation—it warned of the threat of a pandemic several times, including in 2013, 2016, 2018, and even 2019. The Department of Defense did not lag behind in issuing strategic warnings. In 2017, following the MERS outbreak, that department released a report warning of the possibility of a similar outbreak in the United States.[8] Press reports also indicate that the CIA and DIA alerted former president Trump that the virus was making its way to the United States as early as February 2020, before it hit the country.[9] Additional strategic warnings were issued by the NSC's director of medical and biodefense preparedness,[10] the Department of Defense, the Council of Economic Advisers,[11] the Department of Health and Human Services,[12] and the Department of Defense's National Center for Medical Intelligence.[13]

But sometimes, even a strategic warning, good as it may be, is ineffective if decision makers blatantly ignore it. As Lankford, Storzieri, and Fitsanakis have shown, whereas previous administrations—and especially the Obama administration—took the threat seriously and took concrete steps to deal with it, the Trump administration ignored the warnings, did not take concrete steps at the national level, and even shied away from commitments that previous presidents had made.[14]

In 2016, in the wake of the Ebola epidemic, the White House established a department of epidemiology (White House's National Security Council Directorate for Global Health Security and Biodefense), and Beth Cameron was appointed senior director. Although the directorate was not purely an intelligence body, its role was to prepare the United States for the next disease outbreak and prevent a pandemic. As Cameron described, "Our job was to be the smoke alarm—keeping watch to get ahead of emergencies, sounding a warning at the earliest sign of fire—all with the goal of avoiding a six-alarm blaze."[15]

Cameron described collaborating with other federal agencies, monitoring U.S. health threats, including a deadly flu detected in China, yellow fever in Angola, and any biological threat that could pose a significant threat to global health security. "My department was required to prepare the U.S. and the world. In any case, a health emergency,"[16] she said. In other words, the very establishment of the department was an expression of the internalization of the strategic warning that was given to former president Obama regarding a strategic threat that the United States faced.

But in 2017, Donald Trump entered the White House, and within the first year of his tenure, he abolished the department, a decision that turned out to be disastrous.

> It's impossible to assess the full impact of the 2018 decision to disband the White House office responsible for this work. Biological experts do remain in the White House and in the government. But it is clear that eliminating the office has contributed to the federal government's sluggish domestic response. What's especially concerning about the absence of this office today is that it was originally set up because a previous epidemic made the need for it quite clear.[17]

Subsequently, the American president's shaky relationship with the intelligence community, as well as with other authorities—and his tendency to ignore expert opinions when they did not match his simplistic worldview or political aspirations—were revealed to be destructive of the ability of the United States to cope with the pandemic.

In the United Kingdom, too, the issue of the risk of a global pandemic was raised by security and intelligence agencies several times over the preceding decade. In 2010, the UK National Security Risk Assessment document indicated a significant risk to public health due to the possibility of an epidemic outbreak. As part of the United Kingdom's National Security Strategy and Strategic Defense and Security Review, published in 2015, an international pandemic was classified as a Tier 1 national security risk (i.e., a high-risk threat, likely to occur in the next five years). Threats at the same risk level include terrorism, cyber-attacks, international military conflicts, instability in other countries, and natural disasters. In 2017, the British Cabinet published the National Risk Register of Civil Emergencies,[18] which reviewed key risks with the potential for causing significant disruption in the United Kingdom over the following years.

One of these risks concerned the spread of diseases and epidemics, estimating a high probability of the onset of a flu-like or other infectious disease in the short term. The Risk Register anticipated the consequences of such an outbreak as a virus causing as much as 50 percent of the UK population to experience symptoms, which could lead to between 20,000 and 750,000 deaths; significant disruption to essential services, particularly education and health; and severe harm to the economy. Two other documents, the 2018 Biological Security Strategy,[19] and a review of the United Kingdom's national security capabilities for 2018, stated that the chance of an outbreak had increased since previous assessments. The Biological Security Strategy even proposed a framework for a national response—understand, prevent, detect, respond—where the intelligence community and the Ministry of Defense were recognized as responsible for identifying biological terrorist threats.[20] A pandemic outbreak, independent of terror-related threats, was, therefore, in the minds of decision makers. But the responsibility for monitoring and warnings remained rather vague and focused on biological terrorist threats. Thus, the warning regarding the specific threat of a pandemic was not concrete enough.[21]

As far as we know, the British intelligence community has not carried out any systematic assessments or significant intelligence gathering on the subject of health crises. No overt evidence shows that UK intelligence agencies provided early warning to the UK government about the dangers the spread of COVID-19 posed. In addition, although the heads of MI5 (UK Homeland Security Intelligence Service) and MI6 (UK Foreign Intelligence Service) have a seat on the UK Government's Committee on COVID-19, known as the COBRA Commission, it is unclear what role they played in setting government policy regarding risk assessments on emergence of the virus.

OPERATIONAL EARLY WARNING: EPIDEMIOLOGICAL INTELLIGENCE

The second dimension of the analysis is what I call epidemiological intelligence—not to be confused with an epidemiological investigation, which is the domain of public health experts. Epidemiological intelligence is a routine intelligence effort that aims to provide a concrete warning to decision makers about the outbreak of an epidemic; and from the moment it breaks out, to provide decision makers with an up-to-date, relevant picture of the rate and direction of spread. This requires continuous monitoring and appropriate collection tools, because, as we saw in the case of COVID-19, sometimes the pandemic's originating country does not share details of the outbreak quickly and transparently with the international community.

In this sense, Western intelligence agencies, particularly the Five Eyes (FVEY), have maintained relatively close cooperation. The allies have played a key role in mapping and predicting the spread of the coronavirus, as well as trying to assess what is happening in closed countries like China, Iran, and North Korea. U.S. secretary of state Mike Pompeo claimed that the alliance was "incredibly helpful" in understanding the outbreak of the virus and that he had seen "the Five Eyes mechanism work to powerful effect" and was "confident that it did so and is continuing to do so during this challenging time."[22] In addition, former Canadian intelligence officials reported that Canada's intelligence agencies were collaborating with the U.S. intelligence agency NCMI to evaluate the rate of spread of the virus in China.[23]

OTHER SECURITY THREATS

The third dimension of analysis, sometimes not addressed publicly, concerns security threats peripheral to COVID-19. A major issue on the agenda of Western intelligence agencies during the COVID-19 era is cyber security, particularly the fear that interested parties would exploit the general panic to carry out cyber-attacks to steal or manipulate sensitive information—including, for example, stealing data from hospitals, planting malicious software, or disseminating disinformation. In the United Kingdom, for example, the National Cyber Security Center (NCSC), which operates under the GCHQ, issued an official warning that a range of cyber-attacks were carried out during this period, as the attackers took advantage of the state of emergency. In Canada, the Canadian Cyber Intelligence Agency (CSE) has partnered with U.S. intelligence agencies, and a spokesman for the organization confirmed that "in coordination with industry partners, CSE has contributed to the removal of thousands of fraudulent sites or email addresses designed for malicious cyber activity, including those impersonating the Government of Canada."[24]

Along with collaborations between national intelligence agencies, the intelligence services also assisted government bodies, and even private companies, in the field of cyber protection. In Spain, the National Intelligence Center (CNI), the country's central intelligence agency, has dealt extensively with the issue: their actions included strengthening the cyber security of critical infrastructure, with an emphasis on the Ministry of Health, and cooperating with national cyber security agencies and the Ministry of Interior. The center also assisted in cyber protection of companies with significant shares in the economy, especially those negatively impacted by the pandemic, and collaborated with the National Cryptologic Center (CCN) and the National Cybersecurity Institute (INCIBE).[25]

LESSONS LEARNED FROM THE ISRAELI CASE

Perhaps the most extreme example of the involvement of intelligence organizations in public health decision-making processes during the COVID-19 era is the Israeli case.[26] Almost overnight, the Israeli government established the Coronavirus National Information and Knowledge Center to assist in building an intelligence snapshot of the COVID-19 response at the national level. At the time of writing, the center is staffed by dozens of officers and enlisted soldiers, most of them personnel of the Military Intelligence Directorate (AMAN), some stationed at the Ministry of Health and others operating from a distance.

The thousands of documents the center distributes, including daily reports and in-depth studies, are publicly available. In addition, the center prepared documents for review and use by decision makers, such as the "Corona Cabinet" (the committee of ministers responsible for managing the COVID-19 crisis), the Ministry of Health, and the National Security Council. The center deals with three key fields: first, "global" research, for learning from other countries' responses to the virus; second, "Israel" research, for understanding the effects on national public health (i.e., dimensions relating to the spread of the disease); and third, research of all that relates to drugs, tests, and vaccines.

The "global" research is intended to provide decision makers with a global benchmark and case studies that can give both an idea of what might be expected in Israel and a foundation for learning from the experience of other countries. To that end, the center has built a branched open-data collection system that includes open-source intelligence (OSINT), conversations and interviews with researchers and public health professionals around the world, analysis of open databases, and more. To carry out the "Israel" research, the center gained access to the Ministry of Health databases and operated advanced analysis tools from the worlds of big data and AI. This created a serious dilemma: the main intelligence body in the country, which is subordinate to the military and whose job it is to gather information about the country's external enemies, was given full access to databases concerning Israeli civilians. To address this problem, the center, with the help of ethicists, wrote a "code of ethics" and set strict rules for the use of information, as well as for the style of writing, which must avoid expressing opinions or any political evocation.

One might wonder about the added value of imposing such responsibility on an intelligence body, particularly a military intelligence body. Let us begin at the end: The Israeli military intelligence holds a leading role in the Israeli intelligence community.[27] The Military Intelligence Directorate is the largest and most resourceful body in that community, and its intelligence assessments on various issues almost always take precedence in the calculations of Israeli decision makers. Given that the center, chiefly staffed by military intelligence personnel, was given responsibility for collecting, processing, and making accessible information that is part public, part private, it thus realized the ultimate objective of intelligence organizations: a systematic and meticulous process of collecting, processing, and making information accessible to decision makers. Only in one place in the state of Israel—and generally also in other Western countries—is there an organization for whom this process is at its core: the intelligence community.

Thus far the Israeli case presents a forward-thinking perspective of "epidemiological intelligence." But what about the broader perspective, which is not limited to the outbreak of a specific pandemic? For several years, epidemiological research has been conducted in the technological realm of the research division of the IDF's Intelligence Directorate. Although officially the subject was addressed, in practice the directorate dealt with it little, if at all. Thus, it is interesting that in terms of organizational change, the IDF's Intelligence Directorate has succeeded in doing what other intelligence organizations around the world have repeatedly failed to do: transform radically, almost overnight. As early as January 2020, the directorate recognized the alarming potential of the pandemic and sounded the alarm; just a month later, it led the establishment of the Information and Knowledge Center.

Another interesting point relates to the center's audience: decision makers are, of course, at the head of the list, but the Israeli public is also an important consumer, given that public sentiment and behavior have a dramatic impact on the country's ability to manage the pandemic. The center's products are also intended to make accurate data accessible to the public, as well as to public health professionals, such as hospital and laboratory managers.

According to a key architect of the center, a member of the Intelligence Directorate, the idea came up against internal complications. Some in the IDF and the directorate doubted the latter's capability to take on the project; others argued that the directorate should focus on other challenges for which it was solely responsible. Another hurdle was the need to allocate resources—a matter that is never straightforward and always sees internal and external organizational power struggles. A third problem concerned the lack of specific expertise within the directorate; center personnel had no choice but to turn to experts from outside the intelligence community, including physicians, academics, and researchers.

Quite a few lessons can be learned from establishment of the center. Once again, the startup nation has proven that it knows how to take a rudimentary idea and quickly build on it to set up a remarkably functional system. A takeaway lesson for larger, more orderly intelligence organizations is the need for immediate action and the importance of agile initiatives growing from the bottom up. Such a Google-like approach expresses one of the central calls of this book: the need to relax and, sometimes, even eliminate, rigid organizational boundaries to allow for agility and enterprise. Another lesson is the need for intelligence organizations to maintain general ongoing preparedness and, in particular regarding the three core issues at the heart of the new age: the struggle over social consciousness, the technological arms race, and the protection of public health. Although I call for flexibility, creativity, and resourcefulness, as well as for allowing initiatives to grow from the ground up, we must at the same time recognize the fact that large countries cannot always achieve the same outcomes as small countries. Western countries' intelligence services must, therefore, maintain preparedness along the intelligence continuum—from strategic warning to tactical levels—while maintaining a minimum operational capability.

Another important lesson is the way in which the Information and Knowledge Center shattered the traditional concept of the intelligence cycle as an organized framework for intelligence work. The center was not built as a classic intelligence organization; it had no "pure" data collection personnel, no spies, and did not intercept telecommunications. The researchers at the center collected a significant portion of the data themselves. They even wrote the reports themselves and often also distributed them, including giving briefings to the various consumers. The case of the Information and Knowledge Center illustrates the power of publicly available information, but also the great difficulty involved in collecting and processing it into a concrete product, both in terms of the variety of information and the need to contend with large amounts of disinformation.

At the same time, the center demonstrated impressive analytical capability based on quantitative data while applying various mathematical techniques. In doing so, the center once again illustrated the need to include data scientists in intelligence work, as well as the potential inherent in big data in all that relates to solving complex problems. A key lesson here is that through the high exposure of intelligence personnel to civilian technologies and practices, almost overnight, knowledge and capabilities from the forefront of the civilian world were integrated into the intelligence world. These can now be adapted to deal with other threats.

The center's activities were not the only means by which the Israeli intelligence community was involved in the fight against COVID-19. The Mossad was responsible for transporting medical equipment, such as respirators and swabs, from abroad, including through unofficial channels. The responsibility for monitoring the whereabouts of COVID-19 patients and identifying potentially infected individuals was placed on the Israel Security Agency (Shabak/Shin Bet); for this purpose, its powers to collect information, particularly cellular data, were extended—a move approved by Parliament in a speedy and unusual procedure with questionable legal validity. And finally, the IDF intelligence technology units were developing solutions for detection and treatment of the virus—from accessible respirators to the development of algorithms and models to detect and predict infection patterns.

The basic question that we need to ask in the wake of the Israeli case is this: Is the warning about an epidemic outbreak and follow-up after the outbreak even an intelligence mission? This question consists of three sub-questions:

1. Does warning of an epidemic fall under the category of intelligence?
2. In dealing with epidemics, both as part of routine operations and in emergency situations, is the intelligence community neglecting other duties for which it is solely responsible and the expert?
3. In democratic regimes, should intelligence agencies have access to private citizen information, together with the data collection capability to obtain such information?

Here we should address a range of approaches: at one end of the spectrum are those who believe that intelligence should focus on threats of political, security, and military significance, and that the world of intelligence is primarily relevant to these domains. Add to them those who fear the increasing intrusion of intelligence organizations into the lives of individuals, as was evident in the Snowden leaks, for example. The COVID-19 pandemic, in their view, gives government bodies the justification for what they automatically aspire to, involving a deeper intrusion into societal groups to obtain as much data as possible. At the other end are those who claim that intelligence must address everything related to threats to national security, which can, in fact, include epidemics. A related viewpoint comes from those who believe that in the reality of an unprecedented threat, the resources of the entire nation must be harnessed to fight the threat, regardless of their primary purpose. And in this context, there are those who believe that the failure of Western, or at least American, intelligence organizations in the COVID-19 case is the most serious intelligence failure in history.[28]

There is no doubt that intelligence organizations have a relative advantage in dealing with threats of this kind: they have at their disposal an educated workforce, skilled in a variety of fields of knowledge and able to quickly learn new domains of knowledge. This is a workforce with a strong affinity for technology, particularly technologies such as those discussed in this book—big data and AI. All intelligence work is a systematic, orderly process of acquiring, processing, and developing knowledge, and its systems and personnel are accustomed to working in conditions of extreme uncertainty. It is a type of thinking that revolves around supporting decision-making processes and, therefore, is practical in nature. Intelligence organizations, like other organizations engaged in security or saving lives, are also very skilled in shifting from routine to emergency situations.

The most important lesson appears to be the need for a more accurate and precise definition of what falls under the national intelligence umbrella. This is required particularly in light of the complex nature of epidemic-type threats. Traditionally, intelligence deals with the collection and analysis of security-related problems, which excludes issues relating to epidemics unless they are purposely introduced by enemies, such as countries or terrorist organizations.

An interesting point concerns the interface between intelligence agencies and political leadership, especially in light of the disregard—not to mention incompetence—that former president Trump demonstrated in the face of the warnings from his intelligence community. Indeed, decision makers are driven by various considerations; the matter of intelligence, or intelligence warning, is just one of a set of political, economic, and other considerations. But given the consistency and escalation of warnings and in the language used by intelligence personnel, as well as the sequence of epidemics that preceded COVID-19, the question arises as to why President Trump's political leadership—and the British political leadership—ignored the warnings.

Lankford, Storzieri, and Fitsanakis raise a very important question in this context: Does the American IC bear some responsibility for President Trump ignoring its warnings?[29] One answer is related to the shaky relationship between those two parties, and more broadly, the president's blatant disregard for expert opinions that are inconsistent with his own. True, from the beginning of the crisis, the former president challenged the clear facts and data that pointed to a serious crisis, together with the experts who presented these facts. He distorted, lied, and diminished the importance of the data, and when the experts did not align with him, he switched to direct attacks on them. Many senior intelligence officials, such as James Clapper and Susan (Sue) Gordon, testified that the president attacked his intelligence services with allegations such as, "I just do not think what you say is true," or simply canceled intelligence briefings in which he saw no value.[30]

But there is another dimension: the responsibility of the intelligence community itself for the fact that its messages did not permeate. I mentioned earlier the devaluation of the status of intelligence in relation to other visible sources of information, such as mass media, television, and websites. This trend was manifested in full force in the United States during President Trump's term, but it is also evident in other countries. Looking back in light of the analysis of the reports, Lankford, Storzieri, and Fitsanakis pointed to the evolving language of the warnings, which began in the early stages as speculation and built up to clear warnings, with a growing focus on the

United States after initial descriptions of the virus on a global, somewhat abstract, scale.[31]

However, and in part as a result of a lack of sufficient knowledge and poor interorganizational cooperation, the warning remained primarily at the strategic level, without the capability to forecast when it would materialize. It is natural, therefore, that American decision makers tended not to prioritize the pandemic threat over other threats that were perceived as more immediate. The key lesson for intelligence organizations, which are in increasing competition with "other information and insight providers," is that they must learn the way to the hearts of decision makers and be involved in the decision-making process at the strategic level, including making accessible the insights gained through their painstaking work.

And yet, for the sake of fairness, it must be admitted that when decision makers demonstrate broad skepticism in the face of expertise and facts, dismissing them in the decision-making process, the job of intelligence organizations becomes difficult, if not impossible.

Chapter 10

The Five Cs of Intelligence Transformation

An ancient proverb, mistakenly attributed to the Chinese, says "may you live in interesting times." On the face of it, this is meant to bestow a blessing, but that blessing contains irony: "interesting times" implies a chaotic period, full of upheavals and disquiet. Like it or not, intelligence organizations live in interesting times. Humanity is changing before our eyes; and in order to maintain relevance, the organizations must be part of this change. These interesting times are fraught with challenges, but also, for the most part, opportunities.

In the opening of this work, I identified the main trends shaping the intelligence world: breakthrough technological capabilities, originating primarily in the civilian sector, are redefining the intelligence enterprise. New threats, together with the transformation of traditional threats, pose challenges to agencies that are only beginning to understand them. The deluge of high-quality information challenges the perception of truth and expectations from intelligence organizations while raising significant privacy concerns. Added to all these are social changes, including those in the labor market, that require intelligence services to rethink their approach to human resources.

But change is not something that organizations like—especially those that are large and belong to the public sector. Resistance to change stems mainly from human fear of the unknown; and no matter how well-devised and well-founded plans may be, we have no guarantee that the future will pan out as predicted. Most people feel comfortable as long as they are in familiar surroundings, even if these surroundings are not optimal. Any change creates uncertainty that threatens the sense of security and control in certain situations, so resistance to change is expected when individuals, groups, or the whole organization believe that the change may destabilize their existing state of affairs and lead them into dangerous situations that cannot be assessed adequately in advance.[1]

Another impediment to change is related to the need to take advantage of investments already made in the organization. Organizations invest in technological infrastructure; in physical assets such as facilities and offices; in training personnel in methods, procedures, contracts, and much more. Organizational change is perceived as a threat to these resource-intensive investments; and many within the organization fear that the investments made will be wasted, thus taking down the prestige of those who initiated them.[2]

Changes, especially those that are deep and far-reaching, require mutual trust among the various partners in the organization and among external actors involved in the organization's activities. Mistrust leads to inadequate sharing of information, concealment in decision making, and lack of transparency regarding expected courses of action and their intended outcomes. This creates misunderstandings, power struggles, and a lack of dialogue—all of which jeopardize the ability to make significant changes. But sometimes material considerations create resistance to organizational change. Plans may be too ambitious, or they may be based on unsubstantiated forecasts. Sometimes they are ineptly designed, pursuing trends while ignoring organizational resource constraints, or are just too risky.

During the many interviews I conducted in researching for this book, I noticed that only a few interviewees expressed opposition to the idea of a need for a radical change in the intelligence agencies, even though most were former members of intelligence communities. Of course, it is easy to propose a change as an outsider (even if formerly an insider), but the public statements of current senior officials within the intelligence communities (specifically American, British, and Israeli) also support the idea that a dramatic change is needed. This probably indicates the overarching mind-set within the organizations; but it is likely that there are opponents to change whose voices go unheard—because their opinion is unpopular in the current climate, or simply because they voice their opposition in closed circles and not in public.

One way or another, the reader who has reached this concluding chapter must already understand the central claim of this book: The present age necessitates a broad-scale revolution in the intelligence world. Without such a revolution, intelligence organizations will struggle to maintain relevance in decision making at the national level. The changes in the environments in which intelligence systems operate are enormous; and thus, to maintain relevance, the agencies must fit their structures and operations to these changing external environments. This will create a healthy dynamic of partnership, or at least reciprocal design, between the intelligence systems and their environments: As they will adapt themselves, the environment will respond accordingly, and players in the intelligence ecosystem will act in a way that serves intelligence needs (including restrictions on agencies that will ensure that individual freedoms are protected).

The literature identifies two basic strategies by which organizations can create environmental conditions that meet their needs while taking into account the constraints of reality: a choice strategy and an impact strategy.[3] Organizations attempt to select the environments they want for themselves by carefully choosing the basket of products they offer to the environment, how the products are delivered, and so on. This is the choice strategy. Organizations also try to influence their environments in various ways, including through advertisements, propaganda, lobbying, struggling against opponents, and collaborating with other organizations. This is the impact strategy. Despite these systematic efforts, only a few organizations manage to accumulate power to an extent that allows them to dictate the conditions they want to the environment.[4] These select organizations usually have exclusive control over the production of goods or the provision of services that are required by the general public—such as the supply of electricity, fuel, or water; or the supply of a more amorphous public product, such as security. Less influential organizations are forced to make changes to their goals, structures, production methods, human resources, and management methods. These changes are a necessity imposed on organizations attempting to adapt to environmental constraints and dictates, given that these conditions are not selectable or influenceable.

My contention here is that intelligence organizations have, until recent decades, enjoyed a monopoly on knowledge and have, therefore, for the most part, been able to dictate the conditions they desire to the immediate environment. But in a gradual process—that did not start recently but is gaining momentum given the growing popularity of information technology—they are losing ground and therefore must reexamine their two core strategies: choice and impact. The right mix is required: First, within the choice strategy, they must reexamine the intelligence process, the intelligence product, their connection with the intelligence ecosystem, and their relationship with decision makers. This reevaluation will lead to a renewed outlook on the impact strategy: the influence of intelligence systems on their environment, including their central role in tackling the challenges of the present and future, such as the struggle over social consciousness and taking an active part in mitigating climate change impacts.

But first and foremost, a shift in mind-set is required. Fortunately, the intelligence mind-set is already changing, and as I have shown in this book, dramatic transformations are already taking place. A necessary condition for any organizational change is an identified gap between desired performance and existing performance—a gap that current and past intelligence officials have identified, as we saw in chapter 3. This performance gap may be expressed in terms of quantity or quality of outputs, the level of efficiency of various organizational processes, competitiveness, the quality of the organization's resources, and its ability to mobilize resources as required—all the challenges we reviewed in chapter 3. To this gap I will also add the element of anticipation—that is, in light of the technological, political, and social trends reviewed in this work, if the world of intelligence does not adapt, a mismatch between the desirable and existing situations will develop, even in the foreseeable future. This is the anticipated performance gap. Organizations that ignore new trends, such as changes in social values; organizations that glorify past successes without examining their future prospects; and organizations that adopt a policy that rejects decision making until the actual occurrence of events, are organizations prone to anticipated performance gaps. Given the current structure of intelligence organizations and their existing positioning in relation to the external environment, a current performance gap will widen in the future unless these organizations radically change their structure and operations.

However, an objective performance gap is not enough but must be a perceived gap. That is, senior executives in the organization must recognize that the current or expected operation of the organization is unsatisfactory and the situation requires change. Indeed, often the tendency is to wait until the situation is clearly untenable before taking steps to deal with the problem. And even when it becomes clear that change is required, the tendency in most organizations is to try smaller-scale solutions first, instead of risking an in-depth analysis that involves examining alternatives and introducing significant organizational changes. In other words, the typical reaction pattern to performance gaps is to do more of the same: to avoid substantial change. No wonder, then, that major organizational changes are made mainly in times of crisis, when the organization faces real existential danger, even though they may have identified the need for change before the crisis arose. The good news that emerges from analyzing the statements of past and present intelligence professionals, decision makers, and academics is that the current and future performance gap is perceived in all its severity. It seems that the prevailing view within the world of intelligence today, despite a few islands of resistance, is that the structures and operational patterns of intelligence organizations are no longer compatible with the changing environment.

In any organizational reality, and even more so in the current climate of increasing complexity and diminishing regularity, broadscale organizational changes are difficult to implement. All organizations face counterforces, internal and external, that work to prevent or undo major changes. Organizations, let alone government organizations and, within them, security agencies, are by nature conservative creatures that oppose change. Nonetheless, numerous changes are made in organizations all the time, despite the difficulties involved. In fact, the phenomenon of change is so prevalent in today's organizational reality that many identify it as a permanent feature of organizations.

Thus, unlike in the late 1940s, when it was possible to proffer a single-order idea in the form of an intelligence cycle—an idea around which the entire intelligence enterprise was organized—at present, one idea, a grand theory if you will, is no longer conceivable.

Nevertheless, a precondition for any organizational change is the presentation of an idea as to the means that will bring about the required change: any proposal that promises to improve the functioning of the organization. Various ideas for organizational change are reflected in change plans that offer ways to deal with the performance gap, including introducing technological, structural, perceptual, behavioral, or personnel changes. Therefore, instead of proposing a single-order idea that will encompass the entire intelligence enterprise, I will now present five basic principles around which the intelligence revolution must be defined—a framework that I call the five Cs of intelligence transformation. This is only a conceptual framework that includes basic principles required to stand at the heart of any transformative process of intelligence organizations: These principles do not, of course, replace strategic plans rooted in the unique context of each individual intelligence community or even an agency.

PRINCIPLE #1: CONNECTION

This principle focuses on the need to connect intelligence personnel with the machines that assist them in their work. The technologies reviewed in this book—and those that will be developed in the future—obviate certain aspects of the work of intelligence personnel. But it would be wrong to claim that they completely remove the human role in intelligence work. It would be more accurate to argue that the new technologies redefine the places where human thinking has an advantage over algorithmic thinking, creating new spaces for human–machine connection.

To create the right balance in the relationship between human-based intelligence work and machine-based intelligence work, the intelligence professional must develop a deep connection with machines. Intelligence work is increasingly dependent on advanced algorithmic capabilities, and intelligence personnel must use these systems in missions that were, until recently, solely performed by humans. Machines excel in the ongoing race of collecting information, processing it, and identifying patterns and deviations from these patterns—which leads, for example, to issuing alerts. These tasks depend on quantities and a variety of information that no human being—not even a group of people—can collect and process. Intelligence personnel, therefore, need to connect to machines at the deepest level: they must understand principles usually considered the domain of computer or data scientists. They need to understand how databases are built and what information and knowledge can—and cannot—be extracted from them. Intelligence personnel must be connected to systems to direct collection efforts, most of them automated, and to extract the information based on advanced data processing systems. This requires an in-depth understanding of databases and algorithms, including of their capabilities and limitations alike. They must understand the technological capabilities in processing information and assisting in certain aspects of intelligence research. These include, for example, receiving updates on adversaries' capabilities; locating a specific person; detecting transmission changes in electronic systems; and constant and deep monitoring of suspicious activities on social networks.

This is not a trivial challenge. To make the most of the collaboration between man and machine, organizational boundaries must be redefined, including the boundaries between collecting, processing, and research bodies. In the past, intelligence knowledge had to go through the cumbersome and restrictive organizational process of receipt from a sensor, deciphering by a collector, processing by processors, before finally landing on the analyst's desk. The increasing accessibility of machine-based processing systems, along with the increasing availability of publicly accessible information, allows today's analysts to develop a direct connection with the raw data. The organizational separation between collection, processing, and research, which was necessary when each component required a defined skill set, must cease.

Human–machine connection will enable mechanized systems to take the place of intelligence personnel in tasks that until recently were at the core of their professions. For example, those working as processors will be less concerned with filtering and optimizing pieces of information in each discipline. I still remember the long nights I spent as a young intelligence officer cataloging the information that came to my desk: textual searches, followed by contextual (semantic) searches have made this task redundant. Today, artificial intelligence (AI) makes it possible to collect, filter, refine, and cross-reference information better than any human analyst. Machines simply do this faster, more accurately, from a broader and more holistic perspective, over a longer time period, across wider geographical spaces, and all while identifying affinities between many and varied domains, including those that are not visible or understandable to a human analyst. Mechanized systems can also distribute the information among partners and consumers in a way that is more accurately tailored to the needs of the recipient. And last but not least, these days a wide range of technologies is available to intelligence personnel to refine the intelligence product—far beyond reports and presentations.

Intelligence personnel will need to continue to develop conceptual frameworks in order to formulate questions, direct the collection and processing tools, understand and interpret the results and meanings of the findings, and formulate recommendations for action. They should see the advanced technologies reviewed in this book as a set of tools that can improve and streamline the intelligence assessment process without taking humans out of the loop. Machines will make better, more accurate assessments under certain conditions, especially regarding behaviors at the tactical level. But they still cannot provide other important components of the assessment, such as producing a complete intelligence picture, interpreting the complete product according to a tangible context, and making recommendations for action based on that interpretation.

Connecting man and machine thus frees intelligence personnel from the complex operational aspects of collection, processing, and research tasks, and allows them to be positioned where the human brain has an advantage over machines. The fact that automated systems can disseminate information tailored to the needs of a variety of recipients more efficiently, cheaper, faster, and more accurately than can humans, enables intelligence professionals to limit their involvement in distribution to the consumer and focus on dialogue at a deeper level: decision-making in conditions of uncertainty.

Of course, this principle requires identification, screening, and multidisciplinary training of quality personnel. Small-scale, limited training is not sufficient. To this end, the traditional intelligence processes previously mentioned must be fundamentally changed. Intelligence personnel and especially analysts must, as a priority, learn practical tools in the use of advanced information systems, even at the expense of a portion of the time previously devoted to broadening their domain-specific knowledge base. Such a knowledge base is indeed necessary (see Principle #5 below), but at a higher order.

PRINCIPLE #2: COLLABORATION

This principle focuses on the need to develop an intelligence ecosystem that is simultaneously intra-organizational, interorganizational, and extra-organizational. The image of "old-school" intelligence personnel is that of brilliant, sometimes eccentric people, with deep, almost encyclopedic knowledge, who tend to act as lone wolves, roaming intellectual or enemy territory. Think James Bond. But intelligence personnel can no longer be lone wolves. In fact, the key to their success lies in their ability to collaborate—with computers, as noted above, with their counterparts in other units, within and outside the agency to which they belong, and with the intellectual, technological, or operational ecosystem in which they exist.

The idea of collaboration is an extension of the concept of jointness, which developed in the American security establishment in the late 1970s. Jointness then, and particularly in the 1980s, referred to activities, operations, and organizational processes in which two or more military arms took part.[5] The concept of jointness also permeated the civil business sector, mainly thanks to the information revolution that allowed companies and organizations to harness advanced computer applications for their needs and made processing fast and parallel, lowering their costs and making information and knowledge accessible to all. Hierarchical and centralized organizations have given way to flexible and dynamic ones characterized by relatively little bureaucracy and independent units that manage networks of interactions. These organizations, with decentralized, flattened, more networked, and dynamic structures that emphasize the relationships between network nodes, are becoming more broadly accepted.[6]

In the same way, intelligence organizations must venerate the concept of cooperation and expand the connotations of jointness beyond mere coordination of actions. Because the intelligence system is in an ever-changing environment, it must function appropriately: as a dynamic system in which all levels are involved in the processes of developing organizational knowledge and enabling constant organizational change. Of course, this should also include interorganizational and extra-organizational cooperation, given that these types of cooperation can also create spaces in which common knowledge will be produced.

Collaboration can only be possible when the information flows freely between and within the organizations. Autonomy at all ranks is another critical dimension, as it enables collaborative ventures, interfaces, and an open and free flow of information. Mutual trust is another necessary condition for creating constructive collaboration; where trust is lacking, it must be created through empowerment and reward for positive actions. Labor norms and support for cooperation are, therefore, key to advancing this principle.

Collaboration should also be reflected in everything related to the intelligence community's contact with actors in its environment—a matter that requires redefining organizational boundaries and making them more diffuse. Indeed, organizations are essentially social entities with unique characteristics that set them apart from other social systems. To demarcate and differentiate themselves, organizations invest considerable efforts in setting their legal, social, economic, physical, and other boundaries. However, despite the demarcation efforts, organizational boundaries are not clear-cut; areas of overlap, no-man's land, and undefined areas obscure the boundaries between elements within and outside the organization. The boundaries are determined primarily around the actions that distinguish the organization from others, but even in terms of operations, the boundary question is becoming increasingly complex at the present time. Organizations work to implement mergers, joint ventures, and strategic alliances; they share sensitive information and maintain preferred relationships with peer organizations located in interorganizational networks.[7]

This trend of breaking through organizational boundaries—mutual intrusion into others' spheres of control and the blurring of distinctions—must be given significant weight in intelligence communities' visions and strategies. Defining boundaries within ecosystems is a complex matter. In such situations, and at this dynamic time, boundaries should be determined in a relative and context-dependent manner. Intelligence organizations must position themselves as significant players within the intelligence ecosystem: a system of individuals, groups, organizations—a multilayered reality formed through an encounter between numerous systems, each consisting of subsystems and individuals. Building such an ecosystem requires a variety of individuals and systems that, in turn, create many reference points to allow for rapid adaptation of the ecosystem to changing conditions. They must ensure connectivity; that is, the ability to create multiple relationships of dependency and influence. Such an ecosystem should be in a constant state of reformation, as a result of the various bodies learning and changing, thus allowing it to adapt to changing conditions.

The main challenge in this context is setting boundaries with the civilian world. Although the intelligence establishment cannot and should not completely topple the walls that separate it from the civilian world, the characteristics of the new age create cracks in those walls that require the establishment to rethink and reorganize the relationship. This is not a trivial matter. Partnerships with public and private companies, academic institutions, research institutes, and the public pose significant challenges for all parties: sharing sensitive and classified information can lead to a violation of citizens' privacy on the one hand and a risk to intelligence sources on the other. As the scope of cooperation expands, so does the risk of false or misleading information "infiltrating" into the agencies themselves.

But the benefits are not trivial. Deep collaboration will give partners access to areas of knowledge to which accessibility is otherwise limited—through the reciprocal enrichment of knowledge, expertise, and technological capabilities that exist in the private sector. It will also help partners in creative problem solving for issues related to national security, and to achieve resource efficiency and savings. Such a partnership will, further, allow each actor to exploit their relative advantages while effectively sharing risks. In this way, collaboration will help intelligence projects make progress—both discrete and ongoing—quickly, efficiently, and over time.

Although this collaboration will require a clear division of roles and responsibilities, it will also require flexibility and adaptability. The private sector will be able to exploit the advantages of this arrangement, such as progress and development without bureaucratic barriers, while making the

most of its technology and expertise, alongside access to scientific knowledge. The intelligence services will be able to focus on orderly planning, promoting the required legislation (e.g., for the purpose of protecting privacy),
working with decision makers to promote political decisions and continuous
monitoring of the quality of the service.

The many initiatives led by the ODNI—such as In-STeP: The Intelligence
Science & Technology Partnership; Academic Outreach; Public-Private
Analytic Engagement Program; Public-Private Talent Exchange; and the
Trade Association Partners Group—are all significant steps in this direction.

PRINCIPLE # 3: CRITIQUE

This principle focuses on the main cognitive task required of intelligence
personnel: the ability to exercise critical thinking across the intelligence
value chain. If machines will free humans from tasks in which they have no
advantage, the question arises as to where the center of gravity of human intelligence will be. The simple answer, especially when it comes to the complex
analytical stratum of intelligence work, would be to redefine humans' role in
the efforts of revealing secrets, solving puzzles, and cracking mysteries.

Before we move on, it is important to explain the difference between
secrets, puzzles, and mysteries. The distinction between secrets and mysteries
was first proposed by Joseph Nye, who pointed out as early as 1994 that intelligence organizations were increasingly dealing with open-ended questions
that did not have a single factual answer; questions that a single intelligence
report or a collection of quality information could not answer. According to
Nye, the shift that brought these types of questions was related to the collapse
of the relative stability of the Cold War era.[8] However, this approach should
be enhanced by the proposal made by the former head of the research division
of the IDF's Intelligence Directorate, Itai Brun.[9]

Brun proposed a threefold division of secrets, puzzles, and mysteries:
secrets are questions that have a clear factual answer that a technological or
human intelligence sensor can answer. For example, is the tank over a hill
or not? Is the terrorist on his way to a suicide bombing or not? How many
nuclear warheads does North Korea have?

Puzzles are questions that have no definitive answer because they deal with
future developments: Will the Iranian public take to the streets and protest the
rule of the ayatollahs? Will the Chinese continue to enlarge their missile array
in the South China Sea? Will Russian president Putin face a confrontation
with NATO? The answers to these questions are always rooted in a particular
context and in the space between the information available to the observer
and their analytical abilities. The information available to those attempting

to solve these puzzles, of course, includes a factual basis—secrets related to enemy capabilities. But at the end of the day, the answer is evaluative in nature, because even the subject of the study does not know for sure how they will react in real time.

The third category is the mysteries, which are broader questions related to deep processes: Will there be a thawing in relations between North and South Korea? Is the Iranian regime stable? How will climate change affect the global balance of power? In short, these questions have no clear factual answer, and no sensors, of any kind, can gather the information that will answer them with certainty. These are questions to which the answers are interpretive in nature and depend on the context—both concrete circumstances and the observer's perspective.

Let us return to the intelligence professional now. As we move from solving secrets to puzzles to mysteries, the human analytical component grows at the expense of the computer component. It is important to note that dealing with any type of challenge requires a human–machine connection. In an age of advanced technological capabilities, the intelligence professional will be less preoccupied with solving secrets, as machines will be able to collect and process information on a larger scale than any group of people—though secrets sometimes also require abstract thinking and conceptualization of the emerging picture.

Puzzles and mysteries are another matter, as they require high-order human thinking—capabilities that do not yet exist technologically. In the case of puzzles, intelligence personnel can present to decision makers the various possibilities regarding future developments and the likelihood that each will be realized. Such a presentation will assist in conditions of uncertainty and toward addressing future scenarios and represents the core discourse between intelligence professionals and decision makers. This point is more pronounced when it comes to mysteries. Here, too, the intelligence professional must present scenarios as to how processes will evolve, and the likelihood that they will be realized; and here, too, there is a dialogue with decision makers, given that the latter's actions will have a significant impact on the future, and consequently, on the likelihood that scenarios will be realized. However, in the case of both puzzles and mysteries, machines can play an important role (e.g., AI systems that can make complex simulations, hypothesize, and generate new insights).

In other words, especially in the case of strategic issues for which the answer is not absolute but is context-dependent, intelligence personnel are required to formulate a conceptual framework based on key assumptions that they must frequently reexamine. Intelligence practitioners, particularly analysts, will need to focus on the need to understand which questions require an answer and, for each question, what will be considered a relevant answer for decision making in concrete contexts. Any question that goes beyond facts requires a priori assumptions that do not usually evoke second-order thinking. In most cases, we presume that these assumptions are self-evident and do not require interpretation. But in the dynamic new reality, the right questions and the right concepts are not in databases: they are a human product that requires a creative process of thinking, interpretation, and critique. As machines free them from the Sisyphean craft of collecting and processing information, intelligence personnel must focus on frequent examination and reexamination of the perceptual and conceptual frameworks on which the means of collecting, processing, and evaluating intelligence should be based.

Forecasts also illustrate the need for critique. Here, too, the difference between predictive models and scenarios must be clarified. A predictive model is a statistical practice that aims to predict future behavior. The models are produced, today more than ever, using advanced algorithms that analyze huge amounts of data from the past and present to identify patterns. The accuracy of these models tends to improve as the question is more focused and precise. An example of a predictive model is consumer behavior analysis that can identify consumption patterns that are highly likely to emerge in the near future.

Scenarios, on the other hand, are a completely different story. Answers about the future of complex global trends are rarely—if at all—to be found in databases that include information about the past and present. Various models do attempt to find patterns in past events, to formulate them as rules, and to assess what will happen in the future if the patterns are preserved. But in broad questions of a more strategic nature, it is not appropriate to assume that the patterns will be preserved. It is possible to attempt to assess the stability of the Egyptian regime based on hard data on GDP, unemployment, and the price of subsidized products. It is possible, also, to apply economic models that will predict the future development of such data. But what about variables that cannot be understood in the present, let alone in the future, such as the public's willingness to take to the streets and demonstrate? Making assumptions based on such variables is impossible—not only because it is impossible to consider all conceivable variables, but also because it is impossible to predict how these variables will behave in the future. Moreover, there are "black swans"—clearly unpredictable developments with far-reaching and unpredictable consequences. This is where human cognitive ability comes in, for which there is, currently at least, no substitute.

There is no doubt that automated collection, processing, and research technologies are advancing and will continue to do so into the future. In some respects, they will make analytic work redundant. However, they do not remove the need for analysts to formulate conceptual frameworks in order to formulate questions, direct collection and processing tools, understand

and interpret the results and significance of the findings, and formulate rec-ommendations for action for the decision maker. We should, therefore, see the advanced technologies reviewed in this book as a set of tools that can improve and streamline the intelligence assessment process without taking human intervention out of the loop. Under certain conditions, machines can make better, more accurate assessments, especially regarding tactical behav-iors. But they still cannot provide other important assessment components, as discussed under Principle #1: producing a complete intelligence picture, interpreting the picture according to a concrete context, and recommending action arising from the interpretation.

PRINCIPLE #4: CREATIVITY

This principle emphasizes the need for creative, dynamic, and flex-ible thinking that takes advantage of the opportunities that new tech-nologies offer. Creativity is the holy grail of strategy. In every field, from academic research to the business world, everyone is looking for ways to enhance creativity—for the simple reason that the nature of the age we are in requires it. The complexity of the strategic environment is precisely why creative thinking is necessary; the essence of a complex situation lies in the dynamic nature of the relationships, connections, interactions, and depen-dence between the parts and not just in the parts themselves. To gain an in-depth understanding of the relationships, and particularly what they mean in changing circumstances, we must think creatively.[10]

But what exactly is creative thinking? In short, it is a type of thinking that takes into account a wide range of possibilities through cognitive synthesis of existing and potential connections. Creative thinking is holistic, diverse, and horizontal thinking—connecting seemingly unrelated ideas, melding ideas, drawing ideas from different disciplines, and pushing the limits of imagination. Why is it essential in intelligence work? Because intelligence work attempts to understand reality based on partial information. By defini-tion, the future has not yet happened; beyond the partial information we have about it, we must exercise our imagination and assessment skills. Intelligence organizations must mobilize their best creativity to imagine the future reality in which they will operate and act in accordance—starting now.

The need to use imagination is a key part of creativity. Thus, intelligence and planning bodies in Western security establishments have begun to draw on the skills of science fiction writers to better articulate the future security challenges they face. The U.S. Army, for example, has set up a "mad scientist laboratory" that looks creatively at the future battlefield.[11]

Why do intelligence communities struggle with this kind of thinking? After all, they are used to thinking about complex issues. The answer is that, despite all the changes in recent years, they still think in silos—the legacy of the intelligence cycle. Intelligence organizations are still hierarchical, organized by discipline, and the relationships between the various functions are still rigid by nature. Traditionally, the way organizations have dealt with complex challenges has been to break them down, then break the pieces into smaller pieces—all with the aim of simplifying the level of complexity. For example, tackling the Soviet missile challenge required an initial division to collect information, process the information gathered, perform an analysis, and then create a forecast. The collection process is traditionally divided into disciplines, including information obtained by visual, human, or electronic intelligence means. The analysis is also divided into separate functions: one that examines the technological aspects, one that examines military functions, one that examines the political context, and so forth, for every step of the process. This kind of thinking may fit the old world, but it certainly does not fit the new one.

Josh Kerbel proposed an excellent analysis of the intelligence cognitive pathology.[12] He argues that the roots of this narrow thinking lie in four analytical principles, also known as rules of linearity—types of heuristic techniques aimed at preventing bias in intelligence thinking:

- First, assuming that multidimensional challenges are incremental in the sense that the whole is equal to the sum of the parts, one can understand the whole by looking at each component individually before reconnecting all the components to make a whole.
- Second, the assumption that behaviors tend to repeat themselves, and what will happen in the future is, highly likely, a variation on what has happened in the past. This first pair of assumptions encourages analysts to adopt analogy-based thinking and projection from the past to the future.
- Third, an assumption that a causal explanation almost always exists between actions and outcomes, and that such a causal explanation can be revealed. This principle encourages analysts to seek a simple, not to mention simplistic, explanation of cause and effect. This type of thinking leads to first-order results, but not beyond.
- Fourth, we assume that a proportional relationship exists between input and output; that is, that a small act will lead to a narrow result, and a large action will lead to a broadscale result. This principle does not encourage analysts to think outside the context of concrete circumstances, where small actions may result in large-scale results, and vice versa.

But in a complex world with bifurcated connections, Kerbel argues, this thinking is dangerous and stands in opposition to creativity. Complex issues tend to challenge the principles he identified: They do not recur again and again, they are not characterized by clear causal relationships, and they are extremely sensitive to a particular set of conditions. Above all, complex phenomena are far more than the sum of their parts. They consist of sub-phenomena that broaden by virtue of the connections between subcomponents, which can only be understood through a holistic approach and the exercise of creative thought.

This is not just a task for analysts. The entire intelligence community must grapple with these restrictive rules. It should encourage creative thinking that is sometimes inconsistent with the need to toe the line, as is generally required in organizations with rigid hierarchical characteristics. The community must observe the world from a different prism: not of complications but of complexity. It must move away from linear organization, structure, and thinking, as embodied in the cycle of intelligence, and must grasp that creative thinking is sometimes not very efficient and does not necessarily yield immediate results. True, creativity is sometimes a long, cumbersome process that has no guarantee of success and is saturated with failures. A common claim against creativity is that it is usually not based on a predetermined set of replicable actions but, rather, is an expression of a particular mind-set, attitude, and culture, supported by loose processes—and even that its outcomes are not necessarily predefined, rigid, and measurable. But assimilating creative thinking requires, first and foremost, disconnecting the supposed dichotomy between success and failure. Every inventor, every athlete, every politician: everyone knows that the road to success is paved with failures. Consider the words of basketball player Michael Jordan, who many deem to be the greatest athlete of all time: "I've missed more than 9,000 shots in my career. I've lost almost 300 games. Twenty-six times, I've been trusted to take the game-winning shot and missed. I've failed over and over and over again in my life. And that is why I succeed."[13]

Creative thinking embraces failure and sees it as an important part of success. It requires taking calculated and measurable risks and then trying again and again, going through a series of failures from which one can learn, improve, and eventually succeed. This is just how venture capitalists operate: They invest in many initiatives, most of them fail, and only a minority succeed. But in the end, most funds thrive, not only thanks to successful start-ups and technologies, but also owing to those that failed.

The corporate and governmental worlds are structured in such a way that they consist of a set of repetitive and predictable actions. Unfortunately, the principles that sociologist George Ritzer defined still apply, even more than three decades after the publication of the first edition of his book *The*

McDonaldization of Society: rationalization, central control based on a robust bureaucratic mechanism, strictly formulated structures and processes, and a clear and defined division of labor, all fixed in written procedures and protocols.[14] Intelligence communities, on the other hand, need to adopt a more flexible outlook that allows for more independence around the issues that personnel are trying to understand and the problems they are attempting to solve.

Above all, intelligence communities must create a culture of creativity and innovation and ensure that this culture permeates all levels of the intelligence organization. They must allocate resources, tangible (e.g., money) and intangible (e.g., managerial attention), to creative initiatives and those that encourage creative thinking. This culture needs to be formed in collaboration with those for whom such liberated thinking is natural, particularly high-tech companies and research laboratories. It flourishes in the meeting of minds and methods from different worlds (e.g., marketing or gaming, that can be adapted to the intelligence context).

But innovation must also come from within. In this context it is worth noting an idea implemented by the ODNI: lateral innovation—a unit housed within the Transformation and Innovation Office in ODNI's Strategy and Engagement Component. The unit focuses on empowering, accelerating, and maximizing innovation initiatives throughout the intelligence community and other federal agencies, without focusing on one particular agency (this is why the initiative is led by the ODNI). The initiative seeks to overcome bureaucratic barriers through learning and mutual inspiration across all arms of the federal government. The unit helps in-house entrepreneurs and innovators bring initial ideas to maturation quickly, including by identifying relevant players and potential customers, assisting in overcoming difficulties, and prototyping. Through the Intelligence, Science, and Technology Partnership (In-STeP) initiative, the unit gives entrepreneurs and innovators access to advanced technological tools, as well as business practices used within and outside the community.[15]

A final point about creativity is the need for diversity that allows for multiple perspectives on reality. Encouraging the integration of diverse populations is a critical step in breaking down the homogeneity that currently characterizes intelligence communities and promoting a climate of creativity. Here, too, groundbreaking thinking is required to break down accepted conventions regarding professional compatibility.

PRINCIPLE #5: CONTENT EXPERTISE

This principle focuses on the need for intelligence personnel to develop and maintain a deep familiarity with the objects they are observing. Alongside all the relatively "new" principles, the traditional principle of content expertise must be maintained and developed. Among the voices calling for a radical overhaul of the intelligence enterprise, we sometimes miss the voices of those who point to the problematic trend in which intelligence personnel, particularly analysts, are becoming less intimately familiar with their adversaries.[16] In this context, intelligence pundits have produced noteworthy studies in the wake of what they perceive as failures resulting from a lack of sufficient familiarity with other cultures. For example, "Improving Strategic Competence: Lessons from 13 Years of War" (2014) is by a group of analysts who served in various U.S. intelligence agencies. A central contention of that study is that technology cannot replace the long-standing proficiency in culture and language. The study also leveled criticism at the concept of RMA (Revolution in Military Affairs), in which technological control and superiority of information are key points for rapid decision making in military operations. According to the authors, though it proved to be successful in the first Gulf War, it failed miserably in Afghanistan and Iraq. Technological superiority cannot exist alongside deep ignorance of the cultural, social, and political space in which military force is exercised; and in the case of Iraq and Afghanistan, such ignorance led to a failure to achieve strategic goals.[17]

Thus, when discussing characteristics of the intelligence transformation, we must take into account that some current dilemmas also concern the place of expert knowledge in intelligence work, and the fact that many believe that this knowledge is undergoing a dangerous process of devaluation. Degradation of content expertise can lead to impairment of in-depth understanding and intelligence products of reduced value; hence, it is the shortcut to loss of relevance for intelligence bodies, especially the research and analysis arms.[18] In a world where knowledge and analysis tools are available to all, new players are trying to take the place of intelligence organizations: companies, journalists, research institutes, even individuals. Given this context, if intelligence services lose their ability to deeply understand and interpret reality, they lose their relative advantage. Intelligence agencies risk becoming providers of *only* operational and tactical content—dimensions in which they have a clear relative advantage, almost exclusive access to information, and a proven track record of success.

Martin Petersen, a former CIA official, warns of intelligence agents' impending lack of relevance to decision makers. He argues that if intelligence is to assist decision makers, it must supply added value beyond what politicians already know; it must present itself as a source of necessary and credible expertise. The key is the ability to place the intelligence snapshot within a historical framework and context of which most decision makers are unaware, and to demonstrate the significance of that context.[19] Thus, the relative advantage and credibility of intelligence analysts will be built through a systematic study of the histories, thought, literature, and languages of the entities they examine: a long and rigorous process of developing content expertise.

Notes

INTRODUCTION: TECHNOLOGY AND SYSTEMIC CHANGE

1. Ludwig Von Bertalanffy, *General System Theory: Foundations Development Applications* (New York: George Braziller, 2015).

CHAPTER 1

1. Hans De Haan and Jan Rotmars, "Patterns in Transitions: Understanding Complex Chains of Change," in *Technological Forecasting and Social Change* 78, no. 1 (2013): 90–102; Bob De Graaff, "By Way of Introduction: A Systematic Way of Looking at the Future of Intelligence," in *The Future of Intelligence: Challenges in the 21st Century*, eds. Isavelle Duyvesteyn, Ben de Jong, and Joop Van Reijn (London: Routledge, 2014), 1–13.

2. Joshua 2:1, NIV—Bible Gateway, accessed November 1, 2019, https://www.biblegateway.com/passage/?search=Joshua+2:1&version=NIV.

3. Rose Mary Sheldon, *Tinker, Tailor, Caesar, Spy: Espionage in Ancient Rome* (Ann Arbor: University of Michigan Press, 1987); Chester G. Starr, *Political Intelligence in Classical Greece* (Leiden: Brill, 1974), Mnemosyne Supplement 31; R. M. Sheldon, *Intelligence Activities in Ancient Rome: Trust in the Gods, but Verify* (London: Frank Cass, 2005).

4. Owen Connelly, *Blundering to Glory: Napoleon's Military Campaigns* (Lanham, MD: Rowman & Littlefield, 2006).

5. Ibrahim Köremezli, "Shpion vs. Casus: Ottoman and Russian Intelligence in the Balkans during the Crimean War (1853–56)," *Middle Eastern Studies* 50, no. 2 (2014): 192–207.

6. John Hughes-Wilson, *The Puppet Masters: Spies, Traitors, and the Real Forces behind World Events* (London: Cassell Military, 2005).

7. Lee Bartholomew, "Radio Spies: Episodes in the Ether Wars," https://californiahistoricalradio.com/wp-content/uploads//2011/11/spies9eR2006.pdf, 4.

8. Gregory Treverton, "The Future of Intelligence: Changing Threats, Evolving Methods," in *The Future of Intelligence: Challenges in the 21st Century*, eds. Isavelle Duyvesteyn, Ben de Jong, and Joop Van Reijn (London: Routledge, 2014), 33.

9. Ralph Erskine and Michael Smith, *The Bletchley Park Codebreakers: How Ultra Shortened the War and Led to the Birth of the Computer* (London: Biteback, 2011).

10. Christopher Andrew, *For the President's Eyes Only: Secret Intelligence and the American Presidency from Washington to Bush* (New York: HarperCollins, 1996), 42.

11. Huge Sebag-Montifore, *Enigma: The Battle for the Code* (New York: Wiley, 2000).

12. David M. Barrett, *The CIA and Congress: The Untold Story from Truman to Kennedy* (Lawrence: University Press of Kansas, 2017), 10.

13. John Houseman, *Front and Center (1942–1955)* (New York: Simon & Schuster, 1979), 45–46.

14. It existed from 1953 to 1999 and was a U.S. agency devoted to public diplomacy.

15. Office of Strategic Services, *Office of Strategic Services Organization and Functions* (HyperWar Foundation, 1945).

16. Arthur S. Hulnick, "Harold P. Ford, Estimative Intelligence: The Purposes and Problems of National Intelligence Estimating," *Journal of Conflict Studies* 14, no. 1 (1994). Accessed June 23, 2020, https://journals.lib.unb.ca/index.php/JCS/article/view/15167.

17. It was merged with the Office of Weapons Intelligence (OWI) on February 25, 1980, to form the Office of Scientific and Weapons Research. Jeffrey T. Richelson, *The Wizards of Langley: Inside the CIA's Directorate of Science and Technology* (Cambridge, MA: Westview Press, 2002).

18. Jeffrey Richelson, *Spying on the Bomb: American Nuclear Intelligence from Nazi Germany to Iran and North Korea* (Washington, DC: W. W. Norton, 2007).

19. Gregory W. Pedlow and Donald E. Welzenbach, *Central Intelligence Agency and Overhead Reconnaissance: The U-2 and Oxcart Programs, . . . 1954–1974* (New York: W. W. Norton, 2016), 159–60.

20. Matthew M. Aid and Cees Wiebes, eds., *Secrets of Signals Intelligence during the Cold War and Beyond* (London: Frank Cass, 2001), 1–26; Clarence E. Smith, *CIA's Analysis of Soviet Science and Technology* (Central Intelligence Agency, June 28, 2008).

21. L. V. Scott, R. Gerald. Hughes, and Martin S. Alexander, *Intelligence and International Security: New Perspectives and Agendas* (London: Routledge, 2011); CIA, "DCI John McCone Creates the Directorate of Science and Technology" (Central Intelligence Agency, April 30, 2013).

22. Leo Marx and Merritt Roe Smith, *Does Technology Drive History? The Dilemma of Technological Determinism* (Cambridge, MA: MIT Press, 1994).

23. John Patrick Finnegan, *Military Intelligence: A Picture History* (Fort Belvoir, VA: History Office, Deputy Chief of Staff, Operations, U.S. Army Intelligence and Security Command, 1992), 184.

24. Department of the Army, *FM 100–5 Operations* (Washington, DC: Department of the Army, 1993).

25. Richard M. Bridges, *Information Operations: FM 100–6* (Fort Leavenworth, KS: U.S. Army, 1996).

26. U.S. Intelligence Community, *Preparing for the 21st Century: An Appraisal of U.S. Intelligence: Report of the Commission on the Roles and Capabilities of the United States Intelligence Community* (Washington, DC: Government Printing Office, 1996).

27. John Shovelan, "9/11 Commission Finds 'Deep Institutional Failings,'" Australian Broadcasting Corporation, archived from the original on February 21, 2006, accessed February 2, 2007, https://www.abc.net.au/am/content/2004/s1160100.htm.

28. Permanent Select Committee on Intelligence, *IC21: The Intelligence Community in the 21st Century, Intelligence Community Management* (U.S. House of Representatives), accessed September 21, 2021, https://www.govinfo.gov/content/pkg/GPO-IC21/html/GPO-IC21-2.html.

29. Patrick Biltgen and Stephen Ryan, *Activity-Based Intelligence: Principles and Applications* (London: Artech House, 2016), 1–3.

30. James R. Clapper, "The National Intelligence Strategy of the United States of America" (Washington, DC: NIS Publication, 2014).

31. Daniel R. Coats, "National Intelligence Strategy of the United States of America 2019" (Washington, DC: NIS Publication, 2019).

32. David Moore, *Sensemaking: A Structure for an Intelligence Revolution* (Washington, DC: NDIC Press, 2004).

33. Central Intelligence Agency, *Digital Innovation* (Central Intelligence Agency, July 13, 2017).

34. Jason Healey, *A Fierce Domain: Conflict in Cyberspace, 1986 to 2012* (CCSA and the Atlantic Council, 2013).

35. Michael Rusted and Diane d'Angelo, "The Path of Internet Law: An Annotated Guide to Legal Landmarks," *Duke Law and Technology Review* (April 12, 2011).

36. Nate Anderson, "Confirmed: U.S. and Israel Created Stuxnet, Lost Control of It," *Ars Technica*, June 1, 2012.

37. Ellen Nakashima, "Obama to Be Urged to Split Cyberwar Command from NSA." *Washington Post*, September 13, 2016, archived from the original September 14, 2016.

38. Chelsea Locke, *Handbook of European Intelligence Cultures* (Lanham, MD: Rowman & Littlefield, 2018).

39. Cabinet Office and National Security and Intelligence, *Intelligence and Security Committee: Annual Report 2016–2017* (gov.uk, July 23, 2018).

40. House of Lords and the House of Commons Joint Committee on the National Security Strategy, *National Security Capability Review: A Changing Security Environment* (London: House of Lords and House of Commons, 2018).

41. Commonwealth of Australia, *2017 Independent Intelligence Review* (Canberra: Department of the Prime Minister and Cabinet, 2017).

42. Cat Barker, *Intelligence Community Reforms* (Canberra: Parliamentary Library, 2017).

CHAPTER 2

1. CSIS Technology and Intelligence Task Force, *Maintaining the Intelligence Edge: Reimagining and Reinventing Intelligence through Innovation* (Washington, DC: Center for Strategic and International Studies, 2021).

2. NCSC, "FBI and NCSC Release New Movie to Increase Awareness of Foreign Intelligence Threats on Professional Networking Sites and Other Social Media Platforms," Office of the Director of National Intelligence, September 30, 2020. Accessed October 11, 2021, https://www.dni.gov/index.php/ncsc-newsroom/item/2145-nevernight-press-release#:~:text=Inspired%20by%20true%20events%2C%20the,to%20turn%20over%20classified%20information.

3. Edward L. Haugland, *Future Military Intelligence CONOPS and S&T Investment Roadmap 2035–2050: The Cognitive War* (Washington, DC: U.S. Army Intelligence, 2019).

4. Tarun Chhabra, Rush Doshi, Ryan Hass, and Emilie Kimball, *Global China: Technology* (Washington, DC: Brookings, 2020).

5. U.S. House of Representatives Permanent Select Committee on Intelligence, *Chairman Schiff Statement on President Biden Ordering National Intelligence Estimate on Climate Change* (Washington, DC: U.S. House of Representatives Permanent Select Committee on Intelligence, 2021).

6. "Yadlin Amos Sviva ve'Bitachon Leumi," in Kobi Michael, Alon Tal, Galia Linderstrauss, Shira Buckchin, Allon Peles, Dov Hanin, and Victor Weiss (eds.), *Sviva, Aklim ve'Bitachon Leum: Hazit Hadasha le'Israel* (Tel-Aviv: INSS, 2021), 1–14 (Hebrew).

7. Shmuel Eeve, "Mashber Ha'Corona, Asonot Teva ve'Shinui Aklim be'Rey Habitachon Ha'Leumi," in Kobi Michael, Alon Tal, Galia Linderstrauss, Shira Buckchin, Allon Peles, Dov Hanin, and Victor Weiss (eds.), *Sviva, Aklim ve'Bitachon Leum: Hazit Hadasha le'Israel* (Tel-Aviv: INSS, 2021), 35–46 (Hebrew).

8. The White House, *National Security Strategy of the United States of America* (Washington, DC: White House, 2017).

CHAPTER 3

1. Loch K. Johnson and Allison M. Shelton, "Thoughts on the State of Intelligence Studies: A Survey Report," *Intelligence and National Security* 28, no. 1 (2013): 109–20; Stephen Marrin, "Improving Intelligence Studies as an Academic Discipline," *Intelligence and National Security* 31, no. 2 (2016): 266–79.

2. Len Scott and P. Jackson, "The Study of Intelligence in Theory and Practice," *Intelligence and National Security* 19, no. 2 (2004): 139–69; Milo Johns and P. Silberzahn, *Constructing Cassandra: Reframing Intelligence Failure at the CIA, 1947–2001* (Palo Alto, CA: Stanford University Press, 2013).

3. Loch and Shelton, "Thoughts on the State of Intelligence Studies."

4. Burton L. Gerber and Jennifer E. Sims, *Transforming U.S. Intelligence* (Washington, DC: Georgetown University Press, 2005).

5. Gregory F. Treverton, *Toward a Theory of Intelligence: Workshop Report* (Santa Monica, CA: RAND, 2006).

6. See, for example, T. Laasko, *Handbook of Social Media Intelligence*, M-Brain, February 2, 2016, accessed April 6, 2020, https://www.m-brain.com/white-papers /handbook-of-social-media-intelligence/; William J. Lahneman, "The Need for a New Intelligence Paradigm," *Intelligence and Counterintelligence* 23, no. 2 (2010): 201–25; Stephen J. Coulthart, "An Evidence-Based Evaluation of 12 Core Structured Analytic Techniques," *International Journal of Intelligence and Counterintelligence* 30, no. 2 (2017): 368–91; S. Artner, R. S. Griven, and J. B. Bruce, *Assessing the Value of Structured Analytic Technique in the Intelligence Community*, (Santa Monica, CA: RAND, 2016); Lars C. Borg, "Improving Intelligence Analysis: Harnessing Intuition and Reducing Biases by Means of Structured Methodology," *International Journal of Intelligence, Security, and Public Affairs* 19, no. 1 (2017): 2–22; Jack Davis, "Improving CIA Analytic Performance: Strategic Warning," *Sherman Kent Center for Intelligence Analysis, occasional papers* 1, no. 1 (2002).

7. For example, Marcos Degaut, "Spies and Policymakers: Intelligence in the Information Age," *Intelligence and National Security* 31, no. 4 (2016): 509–31; Chandler P. Atwood, "Activity-Based Intelligence—Revolutionizing Military Intelligence Analysis," *Joint Force Quarterly* 77, no. 2 (2015): 24–34.

8. Richard M. Medina, "From Anthropology to Human Geography—Human Terrain and the Evolution of Operational Sociocultural Understanding," *Intelligence and National Security* 31, no. 2 (2016): 137–53; M. T. Flynn, M. F. Pottinger, and P. D. Batchelor, *Fixing Intel: A Blueprint for Making Intelligence Relevant in Afghanistan* (Washington, DC: Center for a New American Security, 2010); Roberto Mugavero, Federico Benolli, and Valentina Sabato, "Challenges of Multi-Source Data and Information New Era," *Journal of Information Privacy and Security* 11, no. 4 (2015): 230–42.

9. Thomas L. Friedman, "Foreign Affairs; World War III," *New York Times*, September 13, 2001, https://www.nytimes.com/2001/09/13/opinion/foreign-affairs-world -war-iii.html.

10. See, for example, IGIS, *Inspector-General of Intelligence and Security: 2017–2018 Annual Report* (Barton, Australia: IGIS, 2018); Department of Defense, *Defense ISR Roadmap, 2007–2017* (Canberra, Australia: Defense Technical Information Center, 2007); Government of Canada, *Strong Secure Engaged: Canada's Defense Policy* (Canberra: Government of Canada, 2021); New Zealand Security Intelligence Service, *New Zealand Security Intelligence Service: Annual Report 2018* (Wellington: New Zealand Government, 2018); Intelligence and Security Committee of Parliament, *Intelligence and Security Committee of Parliament: Annual Report 2017–2018* (London: Intelligence and Security Committee of Parliament, 2018); National Intelligence Strategy, *National Intelligence Strategy of the United States of America: 2019* (McLean, VA: Office of the Director of National Intelligence, 2019); John A. Kringen, "Keeping Watch on the World: Rethinking the Concept of Global Coverage in the U.S. Intelligence Community," *Studies in Intelligence* 59, no. 3 (2015): 1–10; Loch K. Johnson and Allison M. Shelton, "Thoughts on the State of Intelligence Studies: A Survey Report," *Intelligence and National Security* 28, no. 1

(2013): 109–20; H. R. McMaster, Scott D. Berrier, Kevin W. Mangum, and Richard A. Davis, *The U.S. Army Functional Concept for Intelligence: 2020–2040* (Fort Belvoir, VA: Defense Technical Information Center, 2017); Steve Fetter and Chris Fall, *A 21st-Century Science, Technology, and Innovation Strategy for America's National Security* (Washington, DC: White House, 2016).

11. See, for example, the writings of Amy Zegart and Zachery Tyson.

12. William J. Lahneman, *Keeping U.S. Intelligence Effective: The Need for a Revolution in Intelligence Affairs* (Lanham, MD: Scarecrow, 2011).

13. David Moore, *Sensemaking: A Structure for an Intelligence Revolution* (Washington, DC: NDIC Press, 2004).

14. Horst W. J. Rittel and Melvin M. Webber, "Dilemmas in a General Theory of Planning," *Policy Sciences* 4, no. 2 (1973): 155–69.

15. Isavelle Duyvesteyn, Ben de Jong, and Joop Van Reijn, eds. *The Future of Intelligence: Challenges in the 21st Century* (London: Routledge, 2014), 2.

16. Michael Morell and Ellen McCarthy, "Head of State Department's Intelligence Arm on Assessing Foreign Leaders: Intelligence Matters," *Intelligence Matters Podcasts*, 2019, accessed March 11, 2021, https://podcasts.apple.com/uz/podcast/head-state-departments-intelligence-arm-on-assessing/id1286906615?i=1000444085895.

17. Kelsey Reichmann, "3 Space Challenges for the Intelligence Community," C4ISRNET, June 4, 2019, https://www.c4isrnet.com/battlefield-tech/space/2019/06/05/3-space-challenges-for-the-intelligence-community/.

18. Jack Corrigan, "Cyber Threats Are Emerging Faster Than DHS Can Identify and Confront Them," *Defense One*, March 21, 2019, https://www.defenseone.com/threats/2019/03/cyber-threats-are-emerging-faster-dhs-can-address-them-secretary-says/155719/.

19. "Confronting 21st Century Challenges," *IBM Watson Media*, accessed November 2, 2020, http://www.ustream.tv/recorded/114060119?fbclid=IwAR2j08PG3-1ttQ8C0D7l5ZyPKgYTtgtlf7sxXHCbjuxC3j18POy0yCu1CjE.

20. Mike Pompeo, "American Enterprise Institute," (blog) 2019, https://www.aei.org/events/intelligence-beyond-2018-a-conversation-with-cia-director-mike-pompeo-livestreamed-event/?utm_source=paramount&utm_medium=email&utm_campaign=thiessen20180123&utm_term=livestreaminvitation&fbclid=IwAR2eGTayLvUNaTFo8gxmJTJcLiA9yYZ97mSIbHTaWnyXR12OfpR_41b5724.

21. Glenn S. Gerstell, "I Work for N.S.A. We Cannot Afford to Lose the Digital Revolution," *New York Times*, September 10, 2019, https://www.nytimes.com/2019/09/10/opinion/nsa-privacy.html.

22. Amy Zegart and Michael Morell, "Spies, Lies, and Algorithms," *Foreign Affairs*, August 28, 2019, https://www.foreignaffairs.com/articles/2019-04-16/spies-lies-and-algorithms.

23. Paul B. Symon and Arzan Tarapore, "Defense Intelligence Analysis in the Age of Big Data," *Joint Force Quarterly* 79 (2015): 4–11.

24. Hannah Ritchie and Max Roser, "Technology Adoption," *Our World in Data*, October 2, 2017, https://ourworldindata.org/technology-adoption.

25. Dave Evans, *Internet of Things: How the Next Evolution of the Internet Is Changing Everything* (Cisco White Paper, April 2011).

26. Spencer Ackerman and Sam Thielman, "US Intelligence Chief: We Might Use the Internet of Things to Spy on You," *The Guardian*, February 9, 2016, https://www.theguardian.com/technology/2016/feb/09/internet-of-things-smart-home-devices-government-surveillance-james-clapper.

27. William B. Norton, "Internet Transit Prices—Historical and Projected," *Dr. Peering White Paper—Internet Transit Prices—Historical and Projections*, accessed November 2, 2019, http://drpeering.net/white-papers/Internet-Transit-Pricing-Historical-And-Projected.php.

28. James Vincent, "Putin Says the Nation That Leads in AI 'Will Be the Ruler of the World,'" *The Verge*, September 4, 2017, https://www.theverge.com/2017/9/4/16251226/russia-ai-putin-rule-the-world.

29. "HSDL: The Nation's Premier Collection of Homeland Security Documents," *Homeland Security Digital Library*, accessed November 2, 2019, https://www.hsdl.org/.

30. "A Discussion on National Security with DIA Director Robert Ashley," *Center for Strategic and International Studies*, accessed November 2, 2019, https://www.csis.org/analysis/discussion-national-security-dia-director-robert-ashley.

31. Russell E. Travers, "Waking Up on Another September 12th: Implications for Intelligence Reform," *Intelligence and National Security Journal* 31, no. 5 (2016): 746–76.

32. A. Boyed, "The World Is Changing—from Commercially Available GEOINT to COVID19—So the National Geospatial-Intelligence Agency Released a List of Tech Challenges the Agency Needs Help to Overcome," Nextgov, April 29, 2020, accessed June 7, 2020, https://www.nextgov.com/emerging-tech/2020/04/national-geospatial-intelligence-agency-outlines-desired-cutting-edge-tech/165013/.

33. Thomas Fox-Brewster, "Everything We Know About NSO Group: The Professional Spies Who Hacked iPhone with a Single Text," *Forbes*, August 30, 2016, https://www.forbes.com/sites/thomasbrewster/2016/08/25/everything-we-know-about-nso-group-the-professional-spies-who-hacked-iphones-with-a-single-text/#578478073997.

34. Philip H. J. Davies, Kristian Gustafson, and Ian Rigden, *The Intelligence Cycle Is Dead, Long Live the Intelligence Cycle: Rethinking Intelligence Fundamentals for a New Intelligence Doctrine* (London: Brunel Centre for Intelligence and Security Studies, 2013), 56–75.

CHAPTER 4

1. Matthieu Guitton, "Using Biotechnology to Build a Workforce for Intelligence and Counterintelligence," *International Journal of Intelligence and CounterIntelligence* 33, no. 1 (2020): 119–34, https://doi.org/10.1080/08850607.2019.1676038.

2. Larry Dignan, "IoT Devices to Generate 79.4ZB of Sata in 2025, Says IDC: Video Surveillance Will Generate a Lot of Data and Enterprise, Industrial, and Individual Data Will Also Surge," *ZDNet*, June 18, 2019, accessed May 28, 2021, https://www.zdnet.com/article/iot-devices-to-generate-79-4zb-of-data-in-2025-says-idc/.

3. Deloitte, *Technology, Media, and Telecommunications Predictions 2020*, https://www2.deloitte.com/content/dam/Deloitte/at/Documents/technology -media-telecommunications/at-tmt-predictions-2020.pdf.

4. James Lewis, *How 5G Will Shape Innovation and Security* (Washington, DC: Center for Strategic and International Studies, 2018).

5. Tarek Sobh and Khaled Elleithy, *Innovations in Computing Sciences and Software Engineering* (London: Springer Science and Business Media, 2010).

6. It was reported that the DoD is considering splitting the contract between Amazon and Microsoft. Taylor Soper, "DoD Likely to Split JEDI Contract between Amazon and Microsoft, Analyst Says," *GeekWire*, March 14, 2020, https://www.geekwire .com/2020/dod-likely-split-jedi-contract-amazon-microsoft-analyst-says.

7. Billy Mitchell, "CIA Quietly Awards C2E Cloud Contract Possibly Worth Billions," *FEDSCOOP*, November 20, 2020, accessed March 28, 2021, https://www .fedscoop.com/cia-quietly-awards-billion-dollar-c2e-cloud-contract/.

8. Timothy Buennemeyer, "A Strategic Approach to Network Defense: Framing the Cloud," *Parameters* 41, no. 3 (2011): 43–58.

9. IARPA, *Molecular Information Storage*, https://www.iarpa.gov/index.php/ research-programs/mist?id=1077; and Jack Corrigan, "The Intelligence Community Wants to Use DNA to Store Extrabytes of Data: The IC Is Exploring Whether Polymers Could Be the Future of Data Storage," *NextGov*, June 11, 2018.

10. "Big Data: World Market Report," *StrategyR*, November 29, 2021, accessed December 20, 2021, https://www.strategyr.com/market-report-big-data-forecasts-global-industry-analysts-inc.asp.

11. Jeremy Ginsberg, Matthew H. Mohebbi, Rajan S. Patel, Lynnette Brammer, Mark S. Smolinski, and Larry Brilliant, "Detecting Influenza Epidemics Using Search Engine Query Data," *Nature* 457 (2009): 1012–14.

12. Chris Anderson, "The End of Theory: The Data Deluge Makes the Scientific Method Obsolete," *Wired*, June 23, 2008, accessed December 20, 2021, https://www .wired.com/2008/06/pb-theory/.

13. DARPA, *Breakthrough Technologies for National Security*, 2015.

14. RAND, *Big Data, Big Questions*, October 16, 2017, https://www.rand.org/blog /rand-review/2017/10/big-data-big-questions.html.

15. Samuel Smith, "How Much Is Palantir Worth?" *Seeking Alpha*, May 27, 2021, accessed March 28, 2021, https://seekingalpha.com/article/4431750-how-much-is -palantir-worth.

16. Palantir, "Foundational Software of Tomorrow. Delivered Today," *Palantir*, accessed December 20, 2021, https://www.palantir.com/.

17. David Poole, Alan Mackworth, and Randy Goebel, *Computational Intelligence: A Logical Approach* (New York: Oxford University Press, 1998), https://www .cs.ubc.ca/~poole/ci.html.

18. Stuart Russell and Peter Norvig, *Artificial Intelligence: A Modern Approach* (Upper Saddle River, NJ: Pearson, 2010), https://www.cin.ufpe.br/~tfl2/artificial -intelligence-modern-approach.9780131038059.25368.pdf.

19. It is worth mentioning that many believe that machine learning doesn't really mimic human intelligence simply because we still don't really know how human

intelligence works. The use of the term "neural network" could be somewhat mis-leading because our understanding of the brain's neural network is still relatively basic. Further, machine neural networks are a kind of statistical feedback network. The fact that they graphically look like a tent and they have "input" and "output" still doesn't make them similar to the human brain. See John Searle, "Consciousness in Artificial Intelligence," *Talk at Google*, 2015, https://www.youtube.com/watch?v=rHKwIYsPXLg.

20. Michael Growthaus, "An AI Can Now Write Its Own Code," *Fast Company*, April 27, 2018.

21. See "A Robot Wrote This Entire Article. Are You Scared Yet, Human?/GPT-3," *The Guardian*, September 8, 2020, accessed September 15, 2020, https://www.aiwriter.app/; https://www.reddit.com/r/slatestarcodex/comments/hmu5lm/fiction_by_neil_gaiman_and_terry_pratchett_by_gpt3/.

22. PANGU-α Team, "PANGU-α: Large-Scale Autoregressive Pretrained Chinese Language Models with Auto-Parallel Computation," *arXiv:2104.12369*, April 2021, accessed June 21, 2021, https://arxiv.org/abs/2104.12369.

23. Hecate He, "China's GPT-3? BAAI Introduces Superscale Intelligence Model 'Wu Dao 1.0': The Beijing Academy of Artificial Intelligence (BAAI) Releases Wu Dao 1.0, China's First Large-Scale Pretraining Model," *Synced*, March 23, 2021, accessed June 21, 2021, https://syncedreview.com/2021/03/23/chinas-gpt-3-baai-introduces-superscale-intelligence-model-wu-dao-1-0/.

24. Karla Lant, "China, Russia and the US Are in an Artificial Intelligence Arms Race," *Futurism*, September 12, 2017, https://futurism.com/china-russia-and-the-us-are-in-an-artificial-intelligence-arms-race.

25. Greg Allan and Taniel Chan, *Artificial Intelligence and National Security* (Cambridge, MA: Belfer Center of Harvard Kennedy School, 2017).

26. Allan and Chan, *Artificial Intelligence and National Security*.

27. Cortney Weinbaum and John Shanahan, "Intelligence in a Data-Driven Age," *Joint Force Quarterly* 90 (2018): 4–9.

28. "Artificial Intelligence in Medicine," *IBM Watson Health website*, March 12, 2020, https://www.ibm.com/watson-health/learn/artificial-intelligence-medicine.

29. Stephan De Spiegeleire, Matthijs Maas, and Tim Sweijs, *Artificial Intelligence and the Future of Defense: Strategic Implications for Small and Medium-Sized Force Providers* (Netherlands: Hague Centre for Strategic Studies, 2017).

30. Kara Frederick, "How to Defend against Foreign Influence Campaigns: Lessons from Counter-Terrorism," *War on the Rocks*, October 19, 2018, https://goo.gl/vfmrTY.

31. Stew Magnuson, "DARPA to Tackle Fake News Scourge (Updated)," *National Defense*, March 26, 2018.

32. Will Knight, "The Defense Department Has Produced the First Tools for Catching Deepfakes," *MIT Technology Review*, August 7, 2018, https://www.technologyreview.com/2018/08/07/66640/the-defense-department-has-produced-the-first-tools-for-catching-deepfakes/.

33. "New Technology Revealed to Help Fight Terrorist Content Online," *gov.uk*, February 13, 2018, https://www.gov.uk/government/news/new-technology-revealed

-to-help-fight-terrorist-content-online; and James Temperton, "Isis Could Easily Dodge the UK's AI-Powered Propaganda Blockade," *Wired*, February 13, 2018. It is also worth mentioning that Peter Thiel, entrepreneur, venture capitalist, and the founder of Palantir, echoes a similar opinion: he argues that humans tend to change their opinions frequently, and statistics-based machines don't "know" how to deal with such constant changes. Peter Thiel and Blake Masters, *Zero to One: Notes on Startups, or How to Build the Future* (New York: Currency, 2014), https://www.amazon.com/Zero-One-Notes-Startups-Future/dp/0804139296.

34. DARPA, *Active Authentication*, 2013, https://www.darpa.mil/program/active-authentication.

35. Federico Clemente and Stephen Gray, "Artificial Intelligence Could Turn Data Paralysis into Information Analysis," *The Cyberedge*, October 1, 2018.

36. "Global Blockchain Market 2021–2026 by Component, Provider, Type, Organization Size, Deployment, Application, Industry, Geography, Competitive Analysis and the Impact of COVID-19 with Ansoff Analysis," *Research and Markets*, April 2021, accessed May 21, 2021, https://www.researchandmarkets.com/reports/5317225/global-blockchain-market-2021-2026-by.

37. Tim Olson, "Supply Chain," *Blockchain Pulse: IBM Blockchain Blog*, March 6, 2018, https://www.ibm.com/blogs/blockchain/2018/03/blockchain-for-intelligence-supply-chains.

38. Kumaresan Mudliar, Harshal Parekh, and Prasenjit Bhavathanka "A Comprehensive Integration of National Identity with Blockchain Technology," *2018 International Conference on Communication Information and Computing Technology (ICCICT)* (2018): 1–6, https://doi.org/10.1109/ICCICT.2018.8325891.

39. Olson, "Supply Chain."

40. Rosco Kalis and Adam Belloum, "Validating Data Integrity with Blockchain," *2018 IEEE International Conference on Cloud Computing Technology and Science (CloudCom)* (2018): 272–77, https://doi.org/10.1109/CloudCom2018.2018.00060.

41. Tom Simonite, "Microsoft and Google Want to Let Artificial Intelligence Loose on Our Most Private Data," *MIT Technology Review*, 2016.

42. Nathan Dowlin, Ran Gilad-Bachrach, Kim Laine, Kristin Lauter, Michael Naehrig, and John Wernsing, "CryptoNets: Applying Neural Networks to Encrypted Data with High Throughput and Accuracy," *Proceedings of the 33rd International Conference on Machine Learning*, 48 (2016), https://www.microsoft.com/en-us/research/publication/cryptonets-applying-neural-networks-to-encrypted-data-with-high-throughput-and-accuracy/.

43. Spiegeleire, Maas, and Sweijs, *Artificial Intelligence and the Future of Defense.*

44. Jed Pressgrove, "Blockchain in Government Will Boil Down to Policy, Practice," *GovTech*, September 25, 2019, https://www.govtech.com/products/Blockchain-in-Government-Will-Boil-Down-to-Policy-Practice.html.

45. Eleanor Rieffel, "Quantum Supremacy Using a Programmable Superconducting Processor," NASA Ames Research Center, August 2019.

46. Adrian Cho, "IBM Casts Doubt on Google's Claims of Quantum Supremacy," *Science*, October 23, 2019, https://www.sciencemag.org/news/2019/10/ibm-casts-doubt-googles-claims-quantum-supremacy.

47. NASA Quantum Artificial Intelligence Laboratory (QuAIL), NASA Website, June 28, 2018, https://ti.arc.nasa.gov/tech/dash/groups/quail/.

48. Kevin Hartnett, "A New 'Law' Suggests Quantum Supremacy Could Happen This Year," *Scientific American,* June 21, 2019, https://www.scientificamerican.com/article/a-new-law-suggests-quantum-supremacy-could-happen-this-year/.

49. CBInsight, "What Is Quantum Computing?," *CBInsight Research Report,* 2019, https://www.cbinsights.com/research/report/quantum-computing/.

50. Glenn S. Gerstell, "I Work for N.S.A. We Cannot Afford to Lose the Digital Revolution," *New York Times,* September 10, 2019, accessed December 20, 2021, https://www.nytimes.com/2019/09/10/opinion/nsa-privacy.html.

51. Sandra Erwin, "Pentagon Sees Quantum Computing as Key Weapon for War in Space," *SpaceNews,* July 15, 2018, https://spgacenews.com/pentagon-sees-quantum-computing-as-key-weapon-for-war-in-space/.

52. Elizabeth Gibney, "Quantum Gold Rush: The Private Funding Pouring into Quantum Start-Ups," *Nature* 574, no. 7776 (2019): 22–24, https://doi.org/10.1038/d41586-019-02935-4.

53. Gibney, "Quantum Gold Rush."

CHAPTER 5

1. An initial version of this chapter appears in Shay Hershkovitz and David Siman-Tov, "Collaboration between Intelligence and Decision-Makers: The Israeli Perspective," *International Journal of Intelligence and Counterintelligence* 31, no. 3 (2018): 568–92.

2. James A. Barry, Jack Davies, David D. Gries, and Joseph Sullivan, "Bridging the Intelligence-Policy Divide," *Studies in Intelligence* 37, no. 5 (1994); Robert Jervis, "Why Intelligence and Policymakers Clash," *Political Science Quarterly* 125, no. 2 (2010): 85–204; L. Keith Gardiner, "Squaring the Circle: Dealing with Intelligence-Policy Disconnects," *Intelligence and National Security* 6, no. 1 (January 2008): 141–53.

3. Sherman Kent, *Strategic Intelligence for American World Policy* (Princeton, NJ: Princeton Legacy Library, 1966), 200.

4. Kent, *Strategic Intelligence for American World Policy*, 180.

5. Kent, *Strategic Intelligence for American World Policy*, 159–64.

6. Amos A. Jordan and William Jesse Taylor, *American National Security: Policy and Process* (Baltimore: Johns Hopkins University Press, 1981), 148–53.

7. Jack Zlotnick, *National Intelligence* (Washington, DC: Industrial College of the Armed Forces, 1962); Jack Zlotnick, *Bayes Theorem for Intelligence Analysis* (Langley, VA: Central Intelligence Agency, 2012), 43–52.

8. The aforementioned quote is based on Huizinga's testimony to the Murphy Commission. See the commission's full report on the organization of the government for the conduct of foreign policy, "Background and Principal Recommendations," Congressional Library of Congress Research Service, 1975, accessed June 23, 2020, https://digital.library.unt.edu/ark:/67531/metadc993828/.

9. Among the most prominent committees, we should mention the Schlesinger Report (1971), the Rockefeller Commission (1975), and the Church Commission (1976).

10. Willmore Kendall, *The Function of Intelligence* (Cambridge, UK: Cambridge University Press, 2011), 452–53.

11. Roger Hilsman, *Strategic Intelligence and National Decisions* (Westport, CT: Praeger, 1981). Roger Hilsman, "On Intelligence," *Armed Forces & Society* 8, no. 1 (Fall 1981): 129–43; Roger Hilsman, *The Cuban Missile Crisis: The Struggle over Policy* (Westport, CT: Praeger, 1996).

12. Robert Jervis, "What's Wrong with the Intelligence Process?," *International Journal of Intelligence and CounterIntelligence* 1, no. 1 (2008): 39.

13. William J. Brands, "Intelligence and Foreign Policy: Dilemmas of a Democracy," *Foreign Affairs*, January 1969, 288.

14. Linda Robinson, Paul D. Miller, John Gordon IV, Jeffrey Decker, Michael Schwille, and Raphael S. Cohen, *Improving Strategic Competence: Lessons from 13 Years of War* (Santa Monica, CA: RAND, 2014), 44–51.

15. Jack Davis, "Paul Wolfowitz on Intelligence Policy-Relations: The Challenge of Managing Uncertainty," *Studies in Intelligence* 39, no. 5 (1996): 35–42.

16. Robert Gates, *Guarding against Politicization* (Langley, VA: Center for the Study of Intelligence, 1992), 8.

17. Gates, *Guarding against Politicization*, 8.

18. G. Murphy Donovan, *Intelligence Rams and Policy Lions* (Langley, VA: Central Intelligence Agency, 1986), 63–74.

19. Tom Bjorkman, "Increasing CIA's Value Added to the Senior Policymaker," *Studies in Intelligence* 4, no. 2 (1998): 1–4.

20. Robert Cardillo, "Intelligence Community Reform: A Cultural Evolution," *Studies in Intelligence* 54, no. 3 (September 2010): 1–7.

21. Josh Kerbel and Anthony Olcott, "Synthesizing with Clients, Not Analyzing for Customers," *Studies in Intelligence* 54, no. 4 (December 2010): 11–27.

22. Kerbel and Olcott, "Synthesizing with Clients," 17.

23. Kerbel and Olcott, "Synthesizing with Clients," 19–20.

24. Paul R. Pillar, "Intelligence, Policy and the War in Iraq," *Foreign Affairs*, April 2006, 15–27.

25. Isaac Ben-Israel, "Philosophy and Methodology of Intelligence: The Logic of Estimate Process," *Intelligence and National Security* 4, no. 4 (1989): 660–718.

26. Thomas Lowe Hughes, *The Fate of Facts in a World of Men: Foreign Policy and Intelligence-Making* (New York: Foreign Policy Association, 1976), 5.

27. Kerbel and Olcott, "Synthesizing with Clients."

28. Hans Heymann Jr., "Intelligence and Policy Relationships," *Studies in Intelligence* 9, no. 2 (1984): 57–66.

29. Yossi Melman, "Mi Zakuk le'Haaracht Modi'in," *Maariv*, September 11, 2015.

30. Kerbel and Olcott, "Synthesizing with Clients," 21.

CHAPTER 6

1. Ofer Guterman, *Hishtalvut Irguney Modi'in Be'ecosystemim Mekomi'im Shel Hadshanut* (Herzliya: Intelligence Methodology Research Center, 2021) (Hebrew).

2. Kathryn Person, Dylan Cohen, Jonathan Miller, and Fiona Murray, "NSWC Crane Innovation Analysis: Contributing to Regional Innovation Ecosystems," *MIT Innovation Initiative*, May 17, 2019.

3. Kristin Quinn, "Future Framework: The Next NGA West Will Usher the IC into an Era of Open Source Information and Mobility," *Trajectory Magazine*, 1 (2017): 13–17.

4. "The Future of Geospatial Is STL Made," *AllianceSTL,* October 10, 2019, accessed April 13, 2021, https://www.stlouis-mo.gov/government/departments/sldc/media/the-future-of-geospatial-intelligence-is-stlmade.cfm.

5. "St. Louis Developing into a Hub for Geospatial Intelligence," *St. Louis Business Journal*, March 21, 2019; Jacob Barker, "Leveraging NGA, New Plan Sees St. Louis Becoming Hub for Geospatial Sector," *St. Louis Post-Dispatch*, June 23, 2020; Amanda Woytus, "As Work Begins on Next NGA West, the New National Geospatial-Intelligence Agency Campus, GeoFutures Plans for Tomorrow," St. Louis, January 23, 2020, accessed October 12, 2021, https://www.stlmag.com/news/nga-west-campus-geofutures/.

6. Shannon McDonald and Morgan Brennan, "Rockets and Intelligence: The FBI Is Building a $1 Billion Campus in Huntsville, Alabama," *CNBC*, November 14, 2019, accessed April 13, 2021, https://www.cnbc.com/2019/11/14/rockets-and-intelligence-the-fbi-is-building-a-1-billion-campus-in-huntsville-alabama.html.

7. Phillip Thompson, "GCHQ Is Going Where the Talent Is: The Reason behind Intelligence Agency's Manchester Move," gloucestershirelive, July 13, 2019.

8. Jennifer Williams, "Why GCHQ's Spies Are Coming out of the Shadows—And Setting Up Next to a Slug and Lettuce," *Manchester Evening News*, October 20, 2020.

9. Frank James, "Dubai Police Chief '99%' Sure Israel's Mossad Killed Hamas Militant," National Public Radio, February 18, 2010, accessed January 14, 2021, https://www.npr.org/sections/thetwo- way/2010/02/dubai_police_chief_99_sure_mos.html.

10. Allon Sasson, Nicole Negbi, and Adi Lev, *Tachkirim Ezrachi'im Al Eiru'im Bitchoni'im ve'Hashai'im - Zarkor* (Herzliya: Intelligence Methodology Research Center, 2021) (Hebrew).

11. "The Beirut Port Explosion," Forensic Architecture, accessed January 14, 2021, https://forensic- architecture.org/investigation/beirut-port-explosion.

12. Sasson et al., *Tachkirim Ezrachi'im Al Eiru'im Bitchoni'im ve'Hashai'im—Zarkor*.

13. S. Coulthart, M. Maloney, and R. Turley, "Where in the World is Baghdadi? Refining a Methodology for Finding National Security Fugitives," *International Journal of Intelligence, Security, and Public Affairs* (2020): 63–80.

14. Greg Myre, "How Online Sleuths Identified Rioters at the Capitol," *NPR*, January 11, 2021, accessed March 15, 2021, https://www.npr.org/2021/01/11/955513539/how-online-sleuths-identified-rioters-at-the-capitol.

15. Sasson et al., *Tachkirim Ezrachi'im Al Eiru'im Bitchoni'im ve'Hashai'im—Zarkor*.

16. Sunny Jiten Singh, *The U.S. Intelligence Enterprise and the Role of Privatizing Intelligence* (Cambridge, MA: Belfer Center for Science and International Affairs, 2019).

17. Singh, *The U.S. Intelligence Enterprise and the Role of Privatizing Intelligence.*

18. Omri Wexler, "Al Mikur Hutz Bekerev Sochnuyot Ha'modi'in ve'Gufey Bitachon," *Cyber, Modi'in ve'Bitachon* 3, no. 1 (2019): 85–104 (Hebrew).

19. Austin Cook, William Edmiston, Stuart Glenn, Derek Goodwin, Matthew Kaehr, James Nebl, Benjamin Phares, Elizabeth Yang, and Jessica Yeo, *What to Cut and How to Cut? Historical Lessons from Past Reductions in the Intelligence Community* (Washington, DC: Office of the Director of National Intelligence, 2012).

20. Bruce C. Berkowitz and Allan E. Goodman, *Best Truth: Information in the Intelligence Age* (London and New Haven: Yale University Press, 2010), 51–56.

21. Robert Baer, "Just Who Does the CIA's Work?" *Time*, April 20, 2007, http://www.time.com/time/nation/article/0,8599,1613011,00.html.

22. Eric Rosenbach and Aki J. Peritz, *The Role of Private Corporations in the Intelligence Community* (Cambridge, MA: Belfer Center for Science and International Affairs, 2009).

23. Tim Shorrock, "5 Corporations Now Dominate Our Privatized Intelligence Industry," *The Nation*, September 8, 2016, accessed May 1, 2021, https://www.thenation.com/article/archive/five-corporations-now-dominate-our-privatized-intelligence-industry/.

24. Rosenbach and Peritz, *The Role of Private Corporations in the Intelligence Community.*

25. Rosenbach and Peritz, *The Role of Private Corporations in the Intelligence Community.*

26. Jacob Sugarman, "'You Can't Have 100 Percent Security and Also Have 100 Percent Privacy': Key Quotes from the President's Defense of His Government's Secret Surveillance Program," *Salon*, June 7, 2013, accessed May 15, 2021, https://www.salon.com/2013/06/07/you_cant_have_100_percent_security_and_also_have_100_percent_privacy/.

27. Dudi Simantov and Liav Sela, *Tafkid Ha'Modi'in Mul Hashpa'a Zara Al Tahalichim Democrati'im* (Herzliya: Intelligence Methodology Research Center, 2020) (Hebrew).

28. Josh Gerstein, "Clapper's Transparency Plan for Intelligence Community Grinds Forward," *Politico*, October 27, 2015, 27.

29. Office of the Director of National Intelligence, *Principles of Intelligence Transparency: Implementation Plan* (Washington DC: Office of the Director of National Intelligence, 2015).

30. FBI Behavioral Threat Assessment Center, *Lone Offender: A Study of Lone Offender Terrorism in the United States (1972–2015)* (Washington, DC: Federal Bureau of Investigation, 2019).

31. Major A. Yossi Kuperwasser and Dudi Simantov, *Mechuyavut Kehilat Ha'modi'in Kema'arich Leumi La'zibur* (Herzliya: Intelligence Methodology Research Center, 2020) (Hebrew).

CHAPTER 7

1. An initial version of this chapter appears in Shay Hershkovitz, "Crowdsourced Intelligence (CROSINT): Using Crowds for National Security," *International Journal of Intelligence Security and Public Affairs* 22, no. 1 (2020): 42–55.

2. Jeff Howe, "The Rise of Crowdsourcing," *Wired*, June 1, 2006, accessed December 20, 2021, https://www.wired.com/2006/06/crowds/.

3. Daren Brabham, "Crowdsourcing as a Model for Problem Solving an Introduction and Cases," *Convergence* 14, no. 1 (2008): 75–90.

4. Vili Lehdonvirta and Jonathan Bright, "Crowdsourcing for Public Policy and Government," *Policy and Internet* 7, no. 3 (September 2015): 263–67.

5. Glenn Hui and Mark Hayllar, "Creating Public Value in E-Government: A Public-Private-Citizen Collaboration Framework in Web 2.0," *Australian Journal of Public Administration* 69, no. 1 (March 2010): s120–31.

6. "MIT Red Balloon Team Wins DARPA Network Challenge," *DARPA*, December 5, 2009.

7. "DARPA's Shredder Challenge," *DARPA*, 2011.

8. "Behind the Code," *GCHQ*, 2011.

9. Steven Stottlemyre, "HUMINT, OSINT, or Something New? Defining Crowdsourced Intelligence," *International Journal of Intelligence and CounterIntelligence* 28, no. 3 (May 2015): 578–89.

10. Richard Heuer, *Psychology of Intelligence Analysis* (Langley, VA: Center for the Study of Intelligence, 1999).

11. Robert Jervis, *Perception and Misperception in International Politics: New Edition* (Princeton, NJ: Princeton University Press, 1976). https://doi.org/10.2307/j.ctvc77bx3..

12. Shay Hershkovitz and Alina Shkolnikov, "Harnessing Collective Wisdom," *Ivey Business Journal*, September/October 2017.

13. Katia Lobre-Lebraty and Jean-Fabrice Lebrat, *Crowdsourcing: One Step Beyond* (London: Wiley, 2013).

14. Dom Galeon, "A Swarm Intelligence Correctly Predicted Time's Person of the Year," *Futurism*, December 6, 2017.

15. "Hybrid Forecasting Competition," *IARPA*, 2018.

16. For initial ideas pertaining to the use of the concept in the context of public goods see Shay Hershkovitz, "Masbirim Israel: Israel's PR Campaign as Glocalized and Grobalized Political Prosumption," *American Behavioral Scientist* 56, no. 4 (2011): 511–30.

17. Alvin Toffler, *The Third Wave* (New York: Bantam, 1981).

18. Stephen Vargo and Robert Lusch, "Evolving to a New Dominant Logic for Marketing," *Journal of Marketing* 68, no. 1 (2004): 1–17. This then new economy was described by various names: "Co-Creation of Value," "Pro-Am," "Wikinomics," and the term that will be used here, "Prosumption" (see George Ritzer and Nathan Jurgenson, "Producer, Consumer . . . Prosumer?," paper presented at the annual meeting of the American Sociological Association, Boston, 2008).

19. Yiannis Gabriel and Tim Lang, *The Unmanageable Consumer* (London: Sage, 2006).

20. Steve Suranovic, *International Trade: Theory and Policy* (Minneapolis, MN: Open Textbook Library, 2010).

21. Max Weber, *The Vocation Lectures* (Indianapolis, IN: Hackett, 2004), 33.

22. "Mom Aids in Hunting Terrorists Over Web," *Washington Times*, August 8, 2003, accessed February 19, 2021, https://www.washingtontimes.com/news/2003/aug/8/20030808-104401-1189r/.

CHAPTER 8

1. Ken Mitchell and Kyle Talbot, "Activity-Based Intelligence: A Perilous Journey to Intelligence Integration," *esri*, March 13, 2017, accessed August 19, 2020, https://proceedings.esri.com/library/userconf/proc17/tech-workshops/tw_2104-74.pdf.

2. Letitia A. Long, "Leveraging Technology," *Pathfinder: The Geospatial Intelligence Magazine* 9, no. 2 (2011), https://apps.dtic.mil/sti/pdfs/ADA539915.pdf.

3. Patrick Biltgen and Stephen Ryan, *Activity-Based Intelligence: Principles and Applications* (London: Artech House, 2016), 1–3.

4. Catherine Johnston, Elmo C. Wright Jr., Jessica Bice, Jennifer Almendarez, and Linwood Creekmore, "Transforming Defense Analysis," *Joint Force Quarterly* 79 (2015), https://ndupress.ndu.edu/JFQ/Joint-Force-Quarterly-79/Article/621117/transforming-defense-analysis/.

5. Shay Hershkovitz and Roey Tzezana, "Connected Devices Give Spies a Powerful New Way to Surveil," *Wired*, January 19, 2017, accessed August 19, 2020, https://www.wired.com/2017/01/connected-devices-give-spies-powerful-new-way-surveil/.

6. Spencer Ackerman and Sam Thielman, "U.S Intelligence Chief: We Might Use the Internet of Things to Spy on You," *Guardian*, February 9, 2016, accessed August 19, 2020, https://www.theguardian.com/technology/2016/feb/09/internet-of-things-smart-home-devices-government-surveillance-james-clapper.

CHAPTER 9

1. Erik J. Dahl, "Was the Coronavirus Outbreak an Intelligence Failure?" *The Conversation*, June 15, 2020, accessed April 22, 2021, https://theconversation.com/was-the-coronavirus-outbreak-an-intelligence-failure-139450.

2. Dahl, "Was the Coronavirus Outbreak an Intelligence Failure?"

3. Donald Trump, "Remarks at Signing of the Coronavirus Preparedness and Response Supplemental Appropriations Act, 2020," White House, 2020, https://www.whitehouse.gov/briefings-statements/remarks-president-trump-signing-coronavirus-preparedness-response-supplemental-appropriations-act-2020/, accessed March 6, 2020; Donald Trump, "Remarks in Roundtable on Border Security," White House, 2020, https://www.whitehouse.gov/briefings-statements/remarks-president-trump

-roundtable-border-security-yuma-az/, accessed June 23, 2020; P. Bump, "How Trump's Rhetoric on Testing in the US Compared with What Was—or Wasn't—Being Done," *Washington Post*, March 31, 2020, https://www.washingtonpost.com/politics /2020/03/31/how-trumps-rhetoric-testing-us-compared-with-what-was-or-wasnt -being-done/, accessed March 31, 2020.

4. Paul Miller, "How the Intelligence Community Predicted COVID-19," *The Dispatch*, March 26, 2020, https://thedispatch.com/p/how-the-intelligence-community -predicted.

5. National Intelligence Council, *Mapping the Global Future* (Washington, DC: National Intelligence Council, December 2004).

6. National Intelligence Council, *Global Trends 2025: A Transformed World* (Washington, DC: National Intelligence Council, November 2008), 75.

7. National Intelligence Council, *Global Trends 2030: Alternative Worlds* (Washington, DC: National Intelligence Council, December 2012).

8. United States Northern Command, Department of Defense Influenza/Pandemic Response Plan (Colorado Springs, CO: Department of Defense, Peterson Air Force Base, 2017), https //www.scribd.com/document/454422848/Pentagon-Influenza -Response, accessed January 6, 2017.

9. Julia Arciga, "US Intelligence Sounded Coronavirus Alarm in January: WaPo," *Daily Beast*, March 20, 2020, https://www.thedailybeast.com/us-intelligence-agencies -reportedly-sounded-coronavirus-alarm-in-january, accessed March 12, 2020.

10. Lena H. Sun, "Top White House Official in Charge of Pandemic Response Exits Abruptly," *Washington Post*, May 10, 2018, https://www.washingtonpost.com/ news/to-your-health/wp/2018/05/10/top-white-house-official-in-charge-of-pandemic -response-exits-abruptly/, accessed May 10, 2020.

11. Council of Economic Advisors, "Mitigating the Impact of Pandemic Influenza through Vaccine Innovation," White House, September 2019, https://www .whitehouse.gov/wp-content/uploads/2019/09/Mitigating-the-Impact-of-Pandemic -Influenza-through-Vaccine-Innovation.pdf.

12. David Sanger, "Before Virus Outbreak, a Cascade of Warnings Went Unheeded," *New York Times*, March 19, 2020, https://www.nytimes.com/2020/03/19 /us/politics/trump-coronavirus-outbreak.html.

13. Josh Margolin and James Gordon Meek, "Intelligence Report Warned of Coronavirus Crisis as Early as November: Sources," ABC News, April 8, 2020, https://abcnews.go.com/Politics/intelligence-report-warned-coronavirus-crisis-early -november-sources/story?id=70031273, accessed April 8, 2020.

14. Ana Maria Lankford, Derrick Storzieri, and Joseph Fitsanakis, "Spies and the Virus: The COVID-19 Pandemic and Intelligence Communication in the United States," *Frontiers in Communication*, December 3, 2020, https://doi.org/10.3389/ fcomm.2020.582245

15. Beth Cameron, "I Ran the White House Pandemic Office. Trump Closed It," *Washington Post*, March 13, 2020, accessed May 12, 2021, https://www .washingtonpost.com/outlook/nsc-pandemic-office-trump-closed/2020/03/13/ a70de09c-6491-11ea-acca-80c22bbee96f_story.html.

16. Cameron, "I Ran the White House Pandemic Office. Trump Closed It."

17. Cameron, "I Ran the White House Pandemic Office. Trump Closed It."

18. *National Risk Register of Civil Emergencies* (London: Cabinet Office, 2017), accessed May 12, 2021, https://assets.publishing.service.gov.uk/government/uploads/system/uploads/attachment_data/file/644968/UK_National_Risk_Register_2017.pdf.

19. Cabinet Office, "UK Biological Security Strategy," Gov.uk, July 30, 2018, accessed April 23, 2021, https://assets.publishing.service.gov.uk/government/uploads/system/uploads/attachment_data/file/730213/2018_UK_Biological_Security_Strategy.pdf.

20. Cabinet Office, "UK Biological Security Strategy."

21. Michael Chertoff, Patrick Bury, and Kjetil Hatlebrekke, *National Intelligence and the Coronavirus Pandemic* (London: RUSI, 2020).

22. "Secretary Michael R. Pompeo Briefing with Journalists from East Asian and Pacific Media Outlets," U.S. Embassy and Consulate in Thailand, March 30, 2020, accessed April 29, 2021, https://th.usembassy.gov/secretary-michael-r-pompeo-briefing-with-journalists-from-east-asian-and-pacific-media-outlets/.

23. Sam Cooper, "Trudeau Sidesteps Questions on Whether China's Coronavirus Data Is Trustworthy," *Global News*, April 2, 2020, accessed April 9, 2020, https://bit.ly/3aX7ZY3.

24. Phil Gurski, "What Role for Canadian Intelligence during the COVID-19 Crisis?" *Hill Times*, March 30, 2020, accessed April 9, 2020, https://bit.ly/3eb6uHu.

25. J. Travieso, "El CNI Refuerza la Ciberseguridad Ante el Covid-19 para Proteger a Ibex 6 y Gobierno." *La Informacion*, March 18, 2020, accessed April 9, 2020, https://bit.ly/2UW8RX7.

26. This section of the chapter is largely based on Colonel N. Sipuro, *Shel Hamerkaz Le'meida ve'Yeda Lemilchama Ba'corona* (Herzliya: Intelligence Methodology Research Center, 2020) (Hebrew).

27. Dudi Simantove and Shay Hershkovitz, *Aman Yotze La'or* (Tel-Aviv: Maarachot, 2013) (Hebrew).

28. Micah Zenko, "The Coronavirus Is the Worst Intelligence Failure in U.S. History," *Foreign Policy*, March 25, 2020, accessed April 29, 2021, https://foreignpolicy.com/2020/03/25/coronavirus-worst-intelligence-failure-us-history-covid-19/.

29. Lankford et al., "Spies and the Virus."

30. Susan Gordon, "Former Trump Administration Officials on National Security" (Washington, DC: Women's Foreign Policy Group, December 3, 2019), https://www.c-span.org/video/?466944-3/trump-administration-officials-national-security, accessed December 3, 2019.

31. Lankford et al., "Spies and the Virus."

CHAPTER 10

1. Yitzhak Samuel, *Organizational Pathology: Life and Death of Organizations* (London: Routledge, 2010), 51–70.

2. Samuel, *Organizational Pathology*, 71–85.

3. Samuel, *Organizational Pathology*, 1–11.

4. Samuel, *Organizational Pathology*, 21–35.

5. Department of Defense, *Dictionary of Military and Associated Terms* (Washington, DC: Department of the Army and Department of Navy, 1994), 132.

6. Kobi Michael, Dudi Simantov, and Oren Yoeli, "Shiluviut Be'irguney Modi'in," *Cyber, Modi'in ve 'Bitachon* 1, no. 1 (2011): 5–27 (Hebrew).

7. Samuel, *Organizational Pathology*, 1–11.

8. Joseph S. Nye Jr., "Peering into the Future," *Foreign Affairs* (July/August 1994).

9. Itai Brun, *Hamechkar Hamodi 'iny* (Herzliya: Intelligence Methodology Research Center, 2019), 58–59 (Hebrew).

10. Josh Kerbel, "The U.S. Intelligence Community's Creativity Challenge," *National Interest*, October 13, 2014, accessed September 14, 2021, https://nationalinterest.org/feature/the-us-intelligence-communitys-creativity-challenge-11451.

11. "The Army's Next Failed War: Large-Scale Combat Operations," *Mad Scientist Laboratory*, March 31, 2022, accessed September 14, 2021, https://madsciblog.tradoc.army.mil/392-the-armys-next-failed-war-large-scale-combat-operations/.

12. Kerbel, "The U.S. Intelligence Community's Creativity Challenge."

13. Michael Jordan, "Thoughts on the Business of Life," *Forbes*, accessed September 14, 2021, https://www.forbes.com/quotes/author/michael-jordan/.

14. George Ritzer, *The McDonaldization of Society: Into the Digital Age* (London: Sage, 2020).

15. Katherine Tobin, "Meet Lateral Innovation," Office of the Director of National Intelligence, June 26, 2019, accessed September 14, 2021, https://www.legistorm.com/stormfeed/view_rss/1545812/organization/95192/title/meet-lateral-innovation.html.

16. Mark M. Lowental, *The Future of Intelligence* (New York: Polity, 2018).

17. Linda Robinson, Paul D. Miller, John Gordon IV, Jeffrey Decker, Michael Schwille, and Raphael S. Cohen, *Improving Strategic Competence: Lessons from 13 Years of War* (Santa Monica, CA: RAND Corporation, 2014), https://www.rand.org/pubs/research_reports/RR816.html.

18. Michael Milshtein, "Lo Tishtane . . . Hishtane, Tishtane," *Modi'in Halacha Le'Ma'ase* 2 (2017): 59–67.

19. Martin Petersen, "The Challenge for the Political Analyst," *Political Analysis* 47, no. 1 (2003): 49, 51–56.

Acknowledgments

I am grateful for several friends and colleagues who encouraged me not only to start the work, but also persevere with it and publish it.

To my colleagues at the Intelligence Methodology Research Center (IMRC), and especially Yossi Kuperwasser and David Siman-tov, who, without their diligent work and advice, this book could not have been published.

To my assistants, Richard Nederlander, Cygal Pellach, and Shashi Rai, who addressed any request, small or big, with the utmost dedication.

I am grateful to my editors at Rowman & Littlefield, and especially April Snider and Nicole Carty, for their help in bringing this book to life.

To my friends and colleagues at the XPRIZE Foundation, Sparkbeyond, and Riskthinking.ai who contributed to the book in different ways, and especially Zenia Tata and Sagie Davidovich.

To my buddies, Omri Arad and Ted Obenchain, who always had a good word of encouragement.

Finally, I would like to acknowledge with gratitude the support and love of my family—my mother, Shlomit, my wife, Shelly, and my three amazing kids, Shacked, Yotam, and Guy. They kept me going, and this book would not have been possible without them. This book is dedicated to you.

Index

About the Author

Shay Hershkovitz (Ph.D.) is a senior research fellow at the Intelligence Methodology Research Center in Israel. He has more than twenty-five years of experience in the strategy and research industry space, including in the Israeli intelligence community, the private sector, and academia. In the past three decades, he has moved in both practitioner and academic circles, where he has gained extensive knowledge of intelligence, strategy, crowdsourcing, and geopolitical analysis. Hershkovitz is coauthor of *AMAN Comes to Light: Israeli Military Intelligence in the 1950s* (2013) and author of dozens of academic articles. He writes regularly for such U.S. media as Wired, TechCrunch, and TheHill.com and speaks to a variety of audiences.